MW01634974

Luigi Crespi

BONSAI

The complete illustrated guide to growing and caring for miniature plants and trees

TRANSEDITION
BOOKS

This edition published in 1995 by Transedition Books, a division of Andromeda Oxford Limited, 11-15 The Vineyard, Abingdon, Oxfordshire OX14 3PX.

Printed in 1995 in Spain by Fournier A. Gráficas, S. A.

ISBN 1 898250 51 0

Contents

CHINA—PLATE 10.

Published Janʸ 1814, by J. Murray, Albemarle Street.

Introduction and History

Bon(pot) - Sai(tree)

For decades now the western world has been acquainted with bonsai and has learned to appreciate it. However, many find the right approach to the cultivation of these miniature plants and trees hard to achieve, being accustomed to the received ideas of beauty and grandeur as developed by European culture.

The art of bonsai began in China and Japan, where eastern philosophy and ideals, which the westerner may find difficult to understand, guide the mind and hands of the oriental bonsai grower, intent upon shaping a tree and recreating it in miniature, in exquisite perfection.

In terms of western culture, it is difficult to appreciate the involved means of communication which a good bonsai creation contains and develops. We are confronted with an idea of beauty which challenges our own rules and which sets other goals, in particular man's constant desire to penetrate the universe in search of inner peace.

Growing bonsai can be a means of expressing our love for nature, through the rearing of a tree and the sympathy which we feel when we are in close contact with nature. Bonsai lovers transmit something of themselves to their plants almost without realizing it, together with their own understanding of the world. This represents an esthetic and creative dimension where individualism and imagination can have free rein, allowing a happier relationship between people and nature.

Thousands of enthusiasts in Europe have turned to bonsai as a rewarding and satisfying pastime. At the same time the market has discovered the value of bonsai, driven by an ever-increasing demand for indoor greenery from city-dwellers. For these reasons, bonsai plants are becoming increasingly popular in the West as they are particularly adaptable to our life style. The species dealt with here in *Bonsai* are less suited to gardens and terraces, but look best inside the house or apartment. The book deals with the cultivation of indoor bonsai plants in some detail, offering advice and technical help so the best results may be obtained with the minimum of experience.

Approaching the world of bonsai means seeing it first of all with the eye of the botanist and naturalist and then through the sensitivity of the artist.

Color plate from the collection of designs executed in China by the English painter William Alexander, between 1792 and 1794, and published in 1806 under the title The Costumes of China. *The placing of two bonsai within the furnishing scheme can clearly be seen.*

The formation of the word derives from the Chinese *Pen-Jing* and the Japanese *Bon-Sai,* in which *Pen* and *Bon* mean "vessel" and *Sai,* means "tree". Bonsai is therefore a tree cultivated in a vessel (or pot) and for this reason requires specialized treatment.

This characteristic determines the eventual size. Plants which in normal conditions grow to considerable height, as bonsai rarely grow higher than one meter (3 feet), at the same time keeping their original shape. The miniaturization process calls for the plant being given constant attention and for a series of operations to be carried out with great care.

Every bonsai develops as a unique example as growth proceeds. Among the definitions attributed to these plants, "a living work of art" is perhaps the most accurate.

The West has generally believed that bonsai cultivation is originally Japanese. It originated, however, in China at the time of the Ming dynasty. It is probable that bonsai reached Japan during the Heian era. It was at this time that Zen Buddhism began to spread, with its principles of naturalness, simplicity, asymmetry and concentration on the "essentials" being instrumental in the search for deep harmony between man and nature.

In fourteenth-century Japan bonsai were used to decorate altars and later; when they appeared as domestic decoration, they still occupied, as they do today, a special place in the *tokonoma* or "heart" of the household. It is since the turn of this century, that bonsai in Japan has become a true art form. Japan has become the center for the finest bonsai and every year thousands of enthusiasts travel there to see them.

It was at the same time in the West, toward the end of the nineteenth century, that the art and technique of bonsai became known. It was a time of renewed enthusiasm for trading with the Far East. At the Paris World Exhibition in 1889, the European public was able to admire these miniature trees for the first time. In the following year, at the same show, a display of bonsai caught the eye of the first European collector, who bought all the trees on display, his name was Rothschild.

In London, in 1909, a large bonsai show was organized, the first in a long series. In America the first bonsai arrived after the war in the Pacific (1942–45) and the massive Japanese immigration of post-war years was also a major influence.

Throughout the world the number of bonsai amateurs is growing and enthusiasts are often brought together in clubs and associations, with the aim of encouraging the awareness of these miniature pot-plants.

There are meetings, shows, exhibitions and conventions in the United States, Australia, the Far East, Europe and Africa. As a result of all this exchange of experience, bonsai production is being constantly updated.

Vinca (V. major)
(4 years old)

Which plants to choose

To be able to survive indoors, a plant must originate in a latitude where the seasons are practically non-existent, or where there are no significant temperature variations between night and day. Trees or bushes growing in our latitude will quickly die if forced to live indoors.

Trees and shrubs in their natural habitat generally grow their roots deep into the soil in search of nutriment. When grown in bonsai pots, which are usually shallow, the plant is considerably affected by the resultant changes in light, temperature and so on.

From the very many tropical and hardy species, the bonsai enthusiast must select plants with those characteristics which lend themselves best to bonsai treatment. Effectively these are plants with small leaves, with branches which harden quickly; with graceful flowers and with small fruit. Bonsai treatment does not bring about genetic changes and has only a limited influence on the size of flower and fruit. These should develop in proportion to the structure of the miniature tree itself.

Bonsai and its Habitat

Let us now see how it is possible to achieve the best results. First of all we should bear in mind the plant's natural habitat. The factors controlling habitat are: temperature, humidity, and light. To these should be added the growing conditions of each plant species and also the diseases to which it may be prone.

It is wise to treat every plant as an individual, just as we treat our friends who each have their own characteristics, moods and fancies. If you cannot find a bonsai expert for your chosen tree, try to read as much as you can about its species. You and your tree both will benefit from your acquired knowledge and gradual expertise.

Temperature

Tropical and sub-tropical species have differing heat requirements.

Tropical plants should be kept at a constant high temperature – 18° to 24°C (65°–75°F). It would also be advisable to lower their night-time temperature by a few degrees though not lower than 16°C (61°F). These species can be placed quite happily next to a window or above the central heating. However, check your window coverings and blinds because if they are heavy, they may trap the cold penetrating from the outside, and disperse the heat from the window area.

As far as sub-tropical varieties are concerned, it is essential to distinguish between winter and summer.

During the summer months these plants may stay in the open, but must be sheltered from the wind. Later in the year, however, as soon as the night-time temperature drops to 10°C (50°F), they must be brought back inside. They should spend the winter in a situation where the air is fresh, in temperature conditions varying from a maximum of 12°C (54°F) to a minimum of 5°C (41°F). Ideal locations for these plants are conservatories, bedrooms (generally cooler than other areas), and corridors.

During this period growth is interrupted and many species shed their leaves. Many of these plants can adapt to warmer conditions and can support a temperature of one or two degrees more. In this case their growth process is simply slowed down, and deciduous trees shed only a part of their foliage. It is always a good idea, however, to ensure a temperature fall of one to two degrees during the night.

Humidity

The range of tools of every good bonsai grower should include a humidity meter. If the plant is placed in conditions that are too dry, it will suffer. It will quickly lose more water than its roots can absorb, eventually interrupting the exchange of gas between its leaves and the air. In this way growth will also be affected. Achieving the right degree of humidity is a very tricky business, but you will eventually succeed by trial and error.

Humidity requirements vary from species to species. Plants with tough waxy leaves, like the fig, are better protected from the dangers of dryness in the air, than are those with tender and herbaceous leaves, such as the yellow sage.

The ideal humidity level for indoor bonsai is 40–50%. To achieve this, use an electric humidifier; or more simply, place a bowl filled with water close to the bonsai or alternatively an indoor fountain with a gush action. As a further option the plant and its container may be placed in a tray filled with moistened pebbles.

The bonsai should be sprayed daily with water and at least once a month a luke-warm wash in the bath-tub will rid the leaves of dust and allow them to breathe more easily.

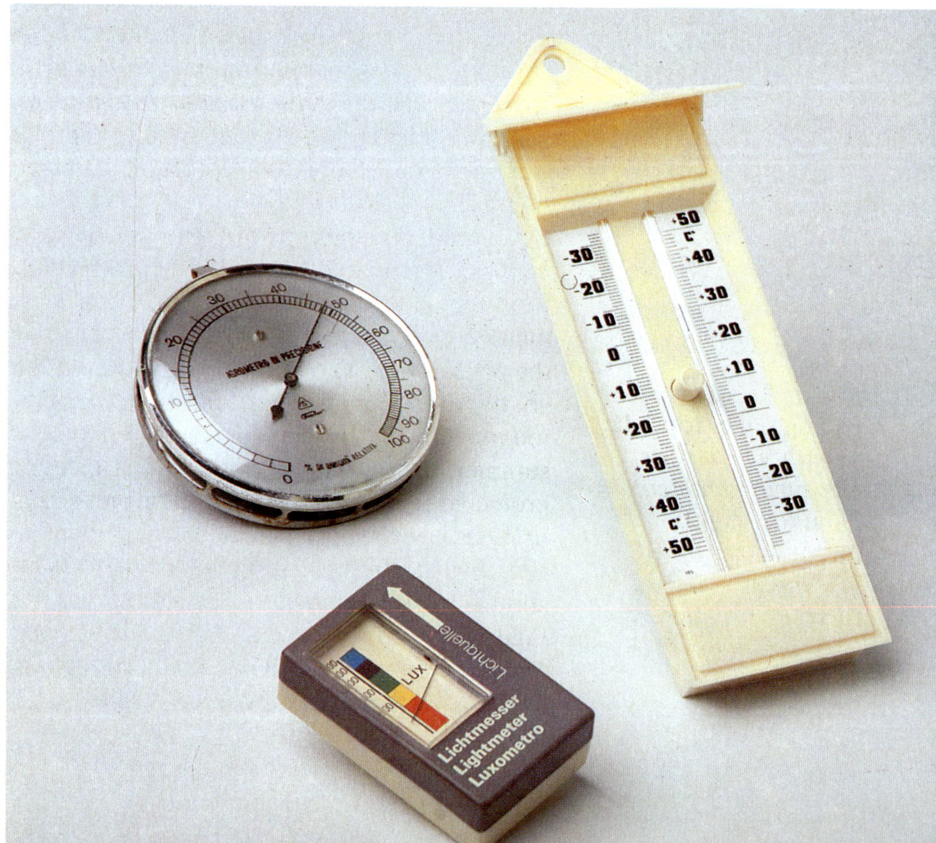

And what about fresh air? In summer your bonsai should suffer no ill effects from fresh air unless it is an extremely tender plant. In winter, however, if you open the windows, you should make sure that the plants are not exposed to direct cold air or harmful drafts.

Light

The correct exposure to light is of primary importance for every plant, and when choosing an indoor location for your bonsai, this matter should be given very special attention.

Do not make the mistake of equating light levels with direct sunlight strengths. The majority of plants will receive harmful effects from being placed in direct sunlight and especially if placed next to glass. The first thing to do is to examine the windows of the chosen area, using a light meter, in order to measure the light-intensity.

During the daytime, most indoor bonsai require as a minimum between 400 and 1000 lux, and some plants need even more. If the natural light is deficient, it can be boosted with artificial light.

However, be careful: normal incandescent lamps are not suitable, in that the light they give out does not correspond to natural light and they can cause lesions and burns on the plants themselves.

Your local light-fitting stockist will be able to advise you what appliances are available for your purpose and, if you seek the advice of a bonsai grower, you will learn much from another's experience.

For aquaria, fluorescent tubes can also be used as well as miniature fluorescent lamps.

According to the type of lamp you are using, it should be placed at a variable distance of between 65 and 80 centimeters (25 and 30 inches) from the plant itself. (If the supports on which they are fixed are painted with white gloss varnish, there can be a saving in the light from the reflectors.) The artificial light should remain turned on for at least six to eight hours per day. Furthermore, if the light is accompanied by too much heat, this can also damage the bonsai. For this reason, in summer, bonsai with a south or west-facing exposure should be protected from the strongest of the sun's rays (blinds or shutters will do or even a newspaper placed between plant and window).

A final recommendation: exposure to light (even when artificial) should be both even and constant; proper well defined rates should be maintained, ideally using automatic switches fitted with timers. If you are an enthusiast with a large collection, glass shelving, equipped with artificial lighting would be the best way to display your bonsai.

Below: *examples of lamps for boosting natural light.*

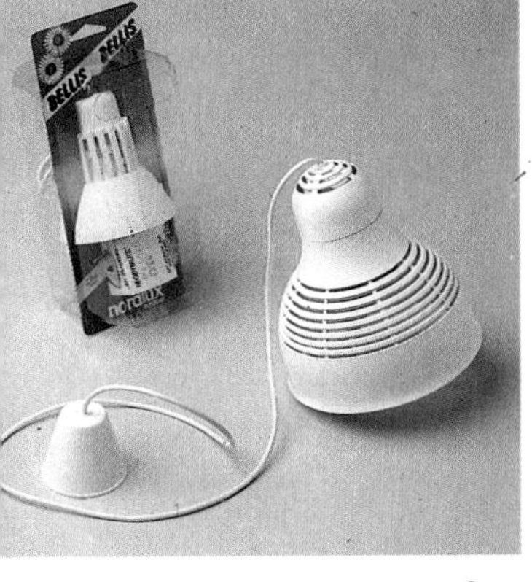

Facing page: **top left:** *humidity meter for measuring ambient humidity,* **right:** *thermometer for measuring temperature,* **below:** *light meter for measuring light intensity.*

Care and Maintenance

A bonsai requires attention, as does every living creature. It is better therefore, that the same person should always look after it. In this way a rhythm and a "natural" routine will be established, with considerable benefit to the plant, and indeed to the grower whose increasing knowledge and experience will create a heightened awareness of the reality of the plant world. After all, this is an, if not the, important aspect of the art of bonsai, creating a partnership between the grower and plant – perfect harmony.

You and your plant will benefit if you draw up a timetable of daily maintenance (checking light, humidity, watering) and periodic (pruning, feeding, re-potting, training and so on).

Watering

It is essential to look every day to see if the bonsai is in need of water. This can be done by checking the state of the soil in the container, bearing in mind that the plant should always be watered before it dries out completely (the lighter the soil is in color, the drier it is). It is preferable to let the water stand at least overnight, before watering the soil or spraying the leaves, to allow any chalky or limestone residues which may be present to filter to the bottom.

The soil should be watered slowly, with brief interruptions, to allow complete permeation. To be sure that the operation is successful, you should be able to see water seeping out of the drainage holes. If the soil is too dry, the water will not be absorbed, and will spill out over the side of the container. Then you should immerse the container in water, leaving it to stand, until any small air bubbles cease rising to the surface.

In the case of plants exposed to the sun, especially during the summer, the "shower" effect, which will tend to damage the leaves, must be avoided. It is better not to spray them, not even during the evening, because if they do not dry out before the onset of the cooler night-time air, they could become more prone to disease from fungal or bacterial attack.

Every plant variety needs a different amount of water; for this reason you should be thoroughly aware of the habits of each individual plant. Also remember that if placed close to the central heating, a bonsai will need more frequent watering, just as during the growing period.

As to the water quality, ideally you ought to know its level of hardness (it should not contain more that 12–15 degrees of hardness and it should be low in chalk or limestone content). Your local water authority will have the relevant information. To soften the water you should simply boil it. Water which is too hard will affect the degree of acidity in the soil and produce chalky deposits. A final piece of advice; in the watering process never use water which is too hot, since this will limit the ability of the plant to absorb nutriment. It would be better to allow the water to stand in the watering-can for at least a few hours.

Fertilization

To enable the bonsai to grow as a healthy and thriving plant, the right fertilizers must be used. This is not always an easy choice; it needs to be approached cautiously, and possibly with the help of an expert (particularly in the case of beginners). Here, therefore, is a little advice which can guide the enthusiast, and avoid causing suffering to the plant either through an excess of fertilizing, or through too little.

Both powder and liquid fertilizers suitable for indoor bonsai are

Various types of watering-can: *long spouts reduce the force of the jet of water, thus promoting better permeation.*

available commercially. The most advisable ones are those in pellet form, as used for outdoor bonsai. Fertilizers can either be applied in the form of salts, that is to say as inorganic fertilizers, or as the organic variety (such as bone meal or powdered horn).

There are available, and indeed in much demand, organic-mineral compounds (always in powder form) involving a combination of both short- and longterm acting fertilizers. Liquid fertilizers are quick-absorbing and therefore more frequently used. Generally it is better to alternate the use of liquid and powder products, paying particular attention however to the amount of the substance which will eventually be administered to the plant. Every species has a different nutritional need and it is, therefore, essential to have the correct information.

All plants however, should be fertilized more frequently during their growing periods but varieties which interrupt growth in the winter do not require extra nutriment during the cold months. Young plants should be helped much more than old ones, just as in the case of the rapid-growth species.

Fertilizer should never be applied just before or after flowering, since the additional energy would go directly to the capillaries and the tree would lose both buds and flowers. No fertilizer should be given after repotting or root-pruning, in order to allow the root system to grow again. In general the period of suspension should last from a month to six weeks.

Before applying the selected fertilizer, within the time-scale appropriate to the plant, the soil must be watered plentifully. Furthermore, in preparing the dosages, always stick closely to the product instructions (generally the quantities as indicated refer to pot-plants; but they will do just as well for bonsai). As a general rule however, it is better to be on the low rather than on the high side. At times an excess of fertilizer can seriously damage a plant which will appear weak and lifeless, as though it has never been fertilized in the first place.

If for any number of reasons (among which could be excessive fertilizing), the roots show signs of sickness, the first thing to do is to suspend fertilization. One of the more obvious signs that the roots may be suffering, is their inability to absorb water. The tree should then be removed from its container, and the roots examined. If these appear fragile; dark in color and damaged, there can be no doubt; they are wasting away due to imperfect nourishment and they should be cut back accordingly. The soil in the container should also be changed and you will need to wait until a healthy root system returns. Only when the plant has started to put out new roots can fertilizing be resumed.

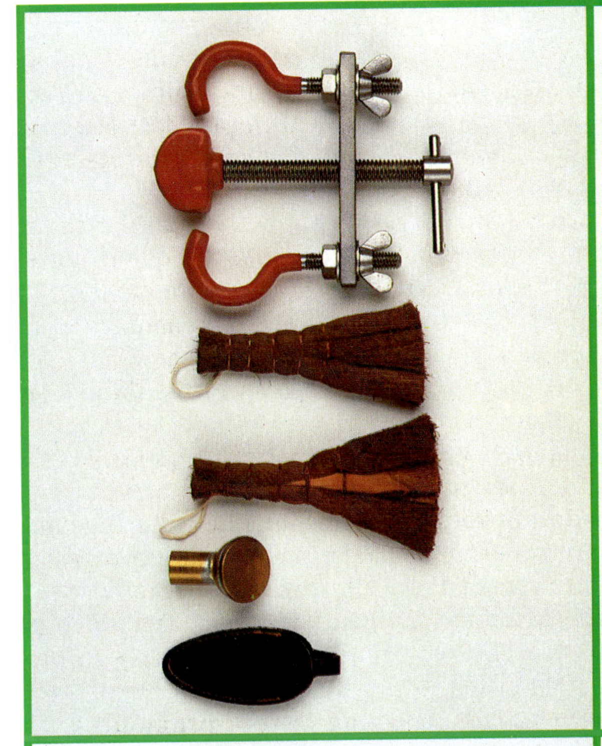

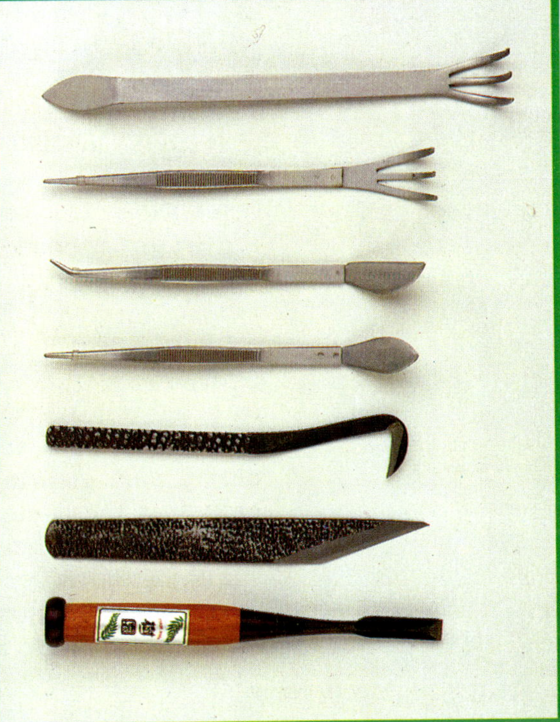

Top left: *brace for stretching trunk and branches; brushes in natural coconut fiber for daily plant maintenance; watering-can nozzles of different sizes to obtain desired spray.*
Top right: *forks for dividing the roots and preparing the bonsai soil foundation for transplanting; knives for cutting weeds away from the roots and for removing unwanted root hairs and splinters; blade with 45° angle; knife with concave blade for cuttings, layering etc; concave chisel for shaping the trunk.*
Bottom left: *slow-yielding organic fertilizers in natural ovule form suitable for bonsai.*

Branch pruning

Once the shape of the bonsai has been decided, you can set about creating it. Firstly you must get hold of the right tools, which should be obtainable in any specialized outlet.

To begin with, you need a pair of bonsai scissors and a pair of scissors for the buds. If the plant intended for reshaping is particularly large, some normal garden-size implement may be necessary. For sealing the pruned ends, appropriate sealants are available commercially.

Although you are free to interpret your plant as you choose, a number of rules do exist of which you must be aware, in order to achieve the right effects of balance and symmetry, without which there could be no bonsai.

For example, the branches which grow on the lower part of the plant, and to the fore, must be cut off. Branches must always grow at the sides and toward the rear. In certain cases, and for esthetic reasons only, exception can be made in the case of smaller branches which may be sometimes allowed in the upper part of the foliage.

In any event, however, branches which grow outward at the same height on the tree must be removed, as well as parallel branches. Branches which embrace or cross over the trunk should also be pruned off, and even those with a door-latch effect.

You should also ensure that the leafy parts of the branches are arranged so as to enable the light to strike them all equally at the same time.

Leaves and shoots

You should pay particular attention when pruning the shoots of an indoor bonsai. Since, in this book, in general, we are dealing with plants of a tropical origin which grow throughout the year, continual pruning is necessary.

The simplest and easiest rule is: only those shoots should remain from which you wish new branches to develop. The effects are immediate: while the lower part of the plant becomes more robust, the branch growth is more delicate. The direction of the only leaf-stalk remaining after pruning has taken place will determine the direction in which the subsequent bud will grow.

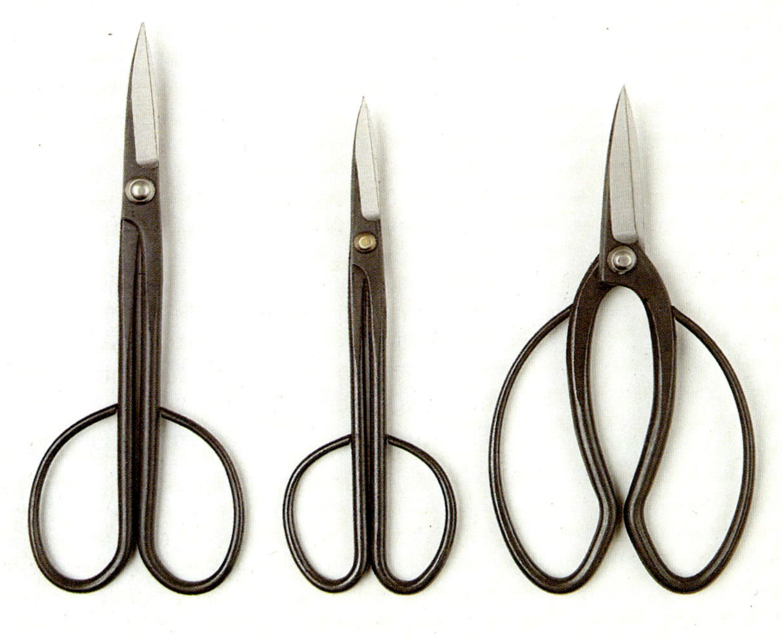

Various types of scissors.
From left to right: *long-handled model for pruning within the foliage; typical pruning model; model suitable for cutting especially strong roots, allowing a perfect cut and immediate root healing.*

Part-concave clippers ideal for pruning smaller branches.

Below: *incorrect and correct pruning.*

Hardy bonsai should be pruned only between March/April and September/October. And, furthermore, if the plant is of a flowering variety, pruning should be carried out only after this has taken place.

As to the leaves, you should remove the largest ones but only during the growing period.

Once a year, between March and August, you should completely remove all the leaves from the plant (ideally doing it in sections over a two-week period). In this way the effect of the late season resting period is simulated but the plant encouraged by the heat will sprout new shoots. The result is that the leaves will become smaller and the branch growth more delicate.

The leaves should always be cut back allowing a small part of the stem to remain.

If you fail to prune the lower branches, this will lead to an enlargement of the trunk. In the same way, if leaves and shoots are not cut back, the lower branches will also increase in girth.

Indoor plants often have aerial roots, which is typically exotic. These plants can also generally be grown as bonsai, provided you select only those which are pleasing to the eye.

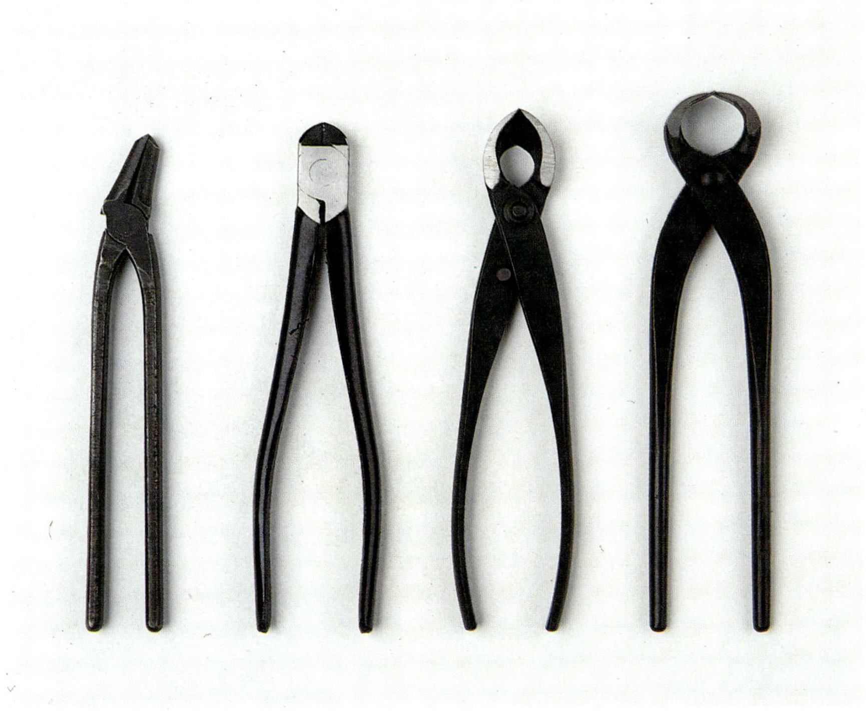

From left to right: *clippers for removal of bark from the branches; clippers essential for removing metal training wire (which is entwined around the branches) without damaging the bark; concave clippers for removing the largest branches and which guarantees perfect sealing of the wound; knob clippers for removing lumps from branches.*

Training wire

For a bonsai to assume the desired shape, it is often necessary to train it by means of external support, using a metal wire. This produces the desired effect more quickly than relying completely on pruning, but the most gentle and sympathetic treatment is called for – a child will not learn to walk happily and confidentally if it is, at first, pushed and shoved about.

Generally indoor bonsai do not need supporting, but due to the spread of the various cultivated species, this practice has in many instances reappeared. The wire can guide the direction of shoot growth and can shape the trunk, in addition to giving it the appearance of age, which results from bending the branches back toward the base of the tree.

Many indoor plants have a particularly delicate bark, which can be damaged if the wire is applied clumsily, or simply too tightly. The same thing can happen if the young tree outgrows its training wire (and indoor bonsai can grow very quickly).

To avoid this, examine the wire and the plant regularly. Should the wire have penetrated the bark you must cut the wire and discard that section which has dug into the bark, rather than inflict ugly scars on the plant by trying to remove it.

The wire is made of copper or anodized aluminum, and varies in thickness depending on which part of the bonsai it is to be used: it is thicker for the trunk and main branches, and finer for the smaller branches and shoots.

Support wire should always be anchored: either to the soil, the trunk, the container, or to another tree. It should be attached in a regular spiral manner, going from bottom to top, and normally starting from the far side of the tree. If you introduce a slight twisting in the direction of the spiral, bending a branch will be easier.

It is essential to avoid binding leaves and buds together. For subjects with a delicate bark strong twine is first used to bend a branch to the required position, with a layer of rubber between it and the support wire.

This is one of the most tricky operations in bonsai, so it must be done with extreme care, step by step, and under the watchful eye of an expert. Time and practice will do the rest. Finally, remember that when you have finished wiring, the bonsai needs a little rest and should not bc placed in direct sunlight. Spray it regularly, and avoid repotting it immediately. Bonsai shapes can also be modified with fine string, or by using small stones or small pieces of wood as props.

You will find that experience is your best guide in developing a wiring technique.

Attach the wire from bottom to top

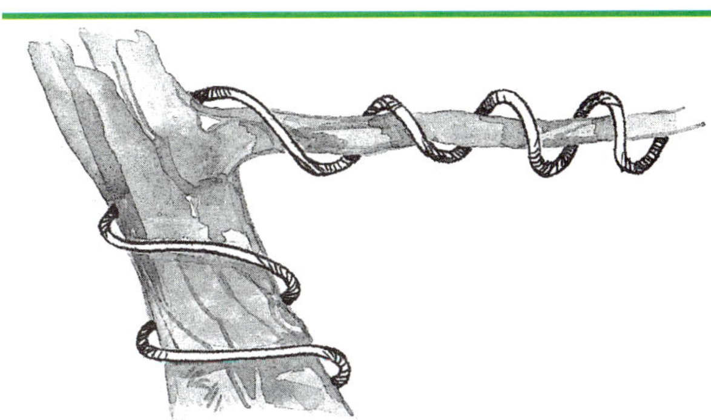

Binding too wide: incorrect method

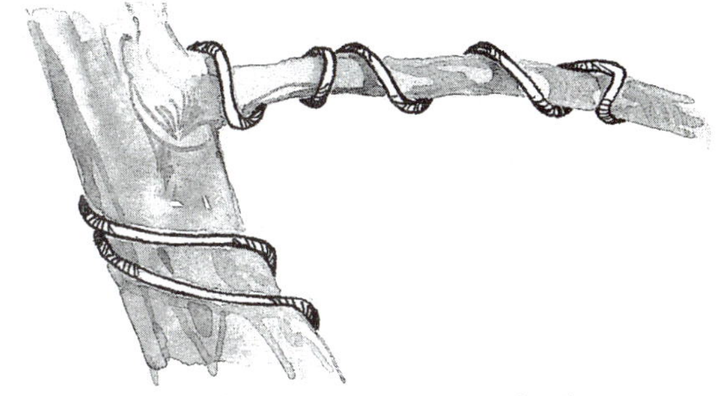

Spirals not uniform: incorrect method

Crossed wire: incorrect method

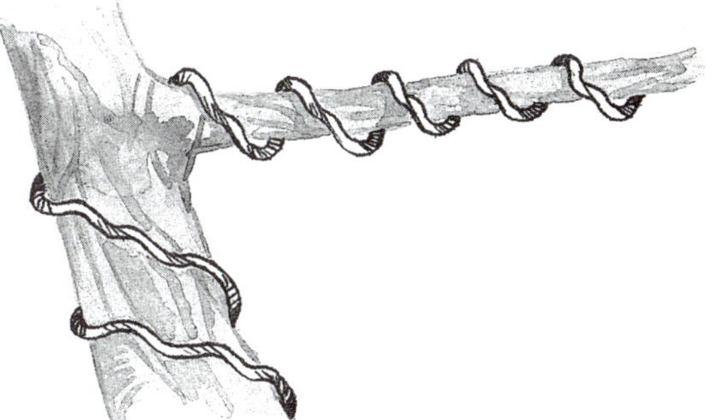

Twisted wire: incorrect method

Do not bind branches and shoots together

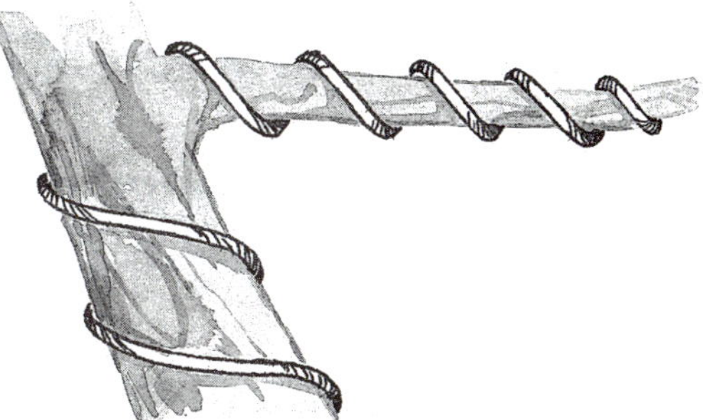

Correct method for wiring

Transplanting and repotting

As with all bonsai, the indoor varieties cannot exist indefinitely in the same soil. In order to have a healthy and thriving plant, the soil in the container must be kept chemically balanced and rich in nutriment. Otherwise, this will become gradually exhausted with the passage of time.

To avoid the plant wasting away the soil must be changed. Normally this is accompanied by cutting back parts of the root system.

Of great importance, is repotting in a container which has to comply with esthetic rules. These must be continually borne in mind, if you wish to act in accordance within the guidelines of structure and proportion, which constitute the beauty and fascination of these "trees in miniature".

Replacing the container is a necessity when the bonsai is a young plant, and growing rapidly. In this instance every year, and at the most every two years, a new container should be substituted, each time about two centimeters(one inch) wider in diameter.

Turning now to the rules for repotting, it is important to remember:

- The younger quick-growing trees should be transplanted every year, while the older slow-growing trees can wait every two to three years. However, the need for this operation is obvious when the roots start to push the soil slightly upward, as they occupy the whole of the soil area.

- The right time for repotting is the beginning of spring, (tropical and semi-hardy bonsai can be transplanted regardless of season).

We can now look in detail at how to carry out this simple but vital operation.

Firstly you must obtain the right compost; mixtures specially prepared for indoor bonsai are available in garden centers. Let the retailer have details of your bonsai variety, and he will supply you with a compost of the right acidity level. Generally the preparation for bonsai is made up of clay or graded akadama soil, sand and humus.

If you wish to produce your own repotting compost, you can do so

Facing page:
Top left and right: *correct method for transplanting.*
Bottom left: *special composts of Japanese origin in varying degrees of calibration which allow oxygenization of the roots, correct drainage and absorption of fertilizer.*
Bottom right: *special scoops for the repotting and soil change processes, and examples of sieves for grading composts.*

TERRA
BONSAI
TERRA
BONSAI
TERRA
BONSAI

using the following formula; two parts peat, one part graded clay, and two parts sand. If, however, the plant requires a particularly acidic soil (for example, azalea), the formula is: one part clayey soil, two parts sand, and five parts peat.

You should ensure that your homemade compost is capable of holding your plant firmly, but that it does not pack down so hard that the roots do not get proper drainage and fertilzation.

As soon as the compost is ready, you can proceed with the actual repotting itself by removing the plant from the container when the soil is at its driest (in this way it will come away from the roots more easily).

After cleaning up the roots, these should be reduced by at least a third; and the dead roots in particular should be cut out. In this way the correct balance and proportion between root system and crown will be maintained, and stronger and more even roots will be produced.

Once this operation is complete, the plant is ready for placing in the container.

This requires special preparation. The drainage holes should be covered with small pieces of plastic mesh fixed with metal wire to prevent the soil from coming through.

If your container is somewhat tall, you should create a separate drainage layer, using pebbles to prevent the water from stagnating. Remember, however, if the container is shallow, not to use compost which is completely peat based as this will not give sufficient support for your plant's roots. If the container is shallow, and you are afraid that your plant may not be getting enough physical support, thread a length of metal wire through the drainage holes and attach the bonsai to it. *(see page 28.)*

Having correctly prepared the base of the container, spread a little compost on it. Then place the plant in the container accordingly, but position it a little off-center. Make sure, however, that the root-base remains above the rim of the pot.

Once you have properly arranged the roots, including any unruly ones, (and you have attached the plant to the metal wire previously inserted), pour in the rest of the compost, prodding it downward with a small stick until it is level and even, and also press it along the edge of the container with your fingers.

Now is the time to water; take care not to break up the soil (the container can be immersed up to halfway in water).

A final piece of advice: do not add fertilizer for at least a month or six weeks, and water less generously than usual.

In terms of the tools and accessories used for this operation, (scissors, prodding-sticks, plastic mesh, metal wire, drainage netting), these are available in all retail outlets specializing in bonsai.

When the plant suffers

In order to keep bonsai healthy, there has to be, as in the case of humans, an effective program for the prevention of sickness and diseases.

When these occur, causing the plant to suffer, you should seek out a commercially available cure. These are now plentiful and increasingly effective.

On the subject of prevention, it is important to remember that this must be a major part of the love, care, and attention which bonsai enthusiasts devote to their plants as they seek to get to know their habits, to adapt to their needs, to site them in the most ideal locations, to feed and to look after them, consistently and with infinite care.

As soon as you are aware of the first signs that all might not be well with the plant, you should try to isolate the cause, with a view to acting immediately and effecting a cure. You should check to see whether there is an excess, or deficiency of humidity, temperature, ventilation, light or nutriment.

For example, a lack of water can cause leaves to dry out, the loss of flowers and buds, and can arrest the plant's growth.

Too much water on the other hand, can disturb the normal functioning of the roots, causing them to rot, at the same time encouraging the spread of parasites.

Mineral deficiencies can cause marks on the foliage; if the leaves turn yellow, this can be due to lack of light or air, or to the presence of pests and diseases.

Pests and diseases

Generally speaking bonsai can be subject to the same pests and diseases which affect trees of the same species growing naturally in the wild. However, if the plant is in good health, it is quite capable of defending itself against parasite attack.

Constant watchfulness is normally enough to foresee, or at least to contain, such attacks. Sometimes, pests and diseases are encouraged by the use of an unsterilized substrate, which allows unwanted guests into the cultivated soil; in some cases pruning that has been carried out with blunt implements will leave jagged cuts which can harbor pests, fungal growth and can easily cause rot to set it.

Garden centers have products to help you eradicate pests and diseases but follow instructions very carefully and adjust proportions to suit miniature plants.

How an indoor bonsai is born

Growing a bonsai, is not only an exquisite form of gardening and a hobby for botany enthusiasts, it is also an art form. These tiny, miniature plants, all energy, balance, and exuberant vitality, differ from a picture or a piece of sculpture, only in as much as they are in a constant state of change. Only if this is fully appreciated can bonsai be nurtured properly indoors.

Many bonsai enthusiasts find that a knowledge of oriental philosophy helps them to a greater understanding of the art. A good book store or library should be able to supply both the beginner and the more advanced grower with books on this subject and also on the principles of Zen.

Having said this, we can now go through the initial steps which are significant in terms of bonsai cultivation, from the moment of decision to grow one of these little trees in our own home.

However, be patient and take your time over selecting your tree, deciding on the container that will suit it best and what shape you want it to achieve. The first move may simply be acquiring a small tree which already has a given shape. On the one hand you may decide to transform an already sizable plant, or you may chose to go about growing it yourself. Whatever your approach, for every bonsai lover the most exciting moments are the first time you chose the right container, work out the future shape of the tree and prune the roots.

Bonsai developed from a plant growing in the wild.

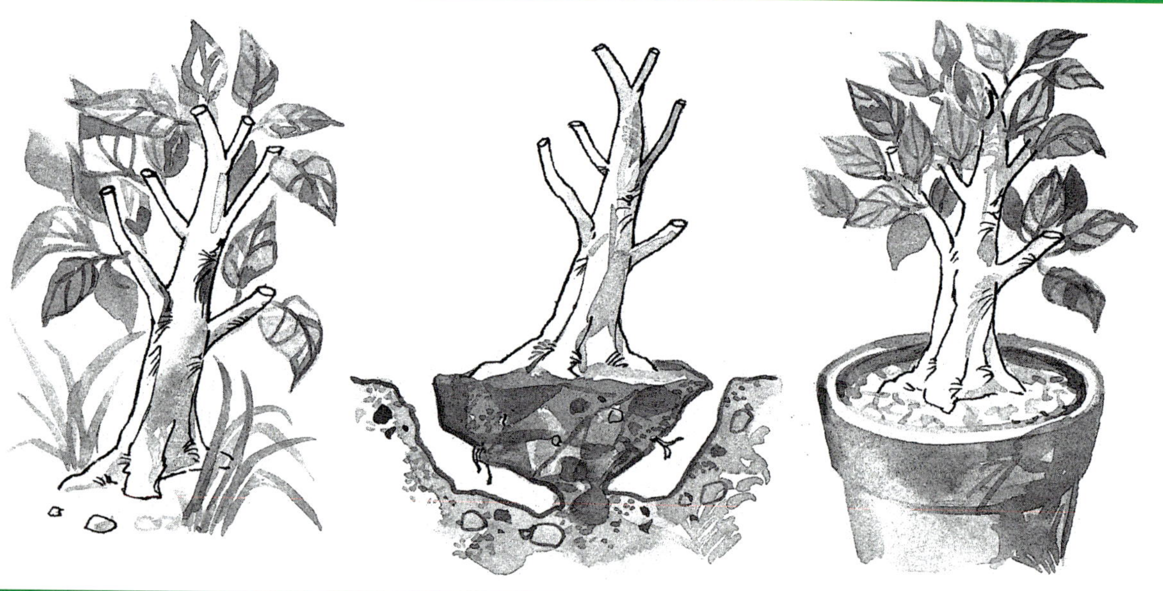

Isolated example of an Aleppo pine. Stretching out over the sea, it harbors typical Mediterranean scrub in the form of undergrowth. In these conditions the trunk takes on a twisted appearance and its branches support an irregular foliage.

Plants in their natural state

It is probably advisable for beginners to learn the early stages of bonsai treatment and cultivation on plants that are sold expressly for the purpose. However, once they have gained some experience and feel more confident – in fact, have become enthusiasts – it is very satisfying to create a bonsai from seedling trees or shrubs found growing in their natural habitat.

The complete bonsai could be a representation in miniature of the landscape in which the seedlings were found; or the seedlings used to achieve a traditional bonsai style – the possibilities are endless. Coastal areas, hedgerows, moorlands and woodlands are a huge nature reserve of bonsai in rough outline from which you can pick out interesting seedlings. If you have selected well, these seedlings, when subjected to bonsai treatment, may yield excellent results.

It is important, however, to bear in mind that in many areas there may be laws prohibiting the removal of plants growing in the wild. It is wise, therefore, to seek permission from the land owner or to make inquiries of the local naturalists' society.

Assuming all is in order and you have selected your seedlings, great care must be taken while unearthing them so that they continue healthy and sturdy specimens suitable for bonsai treatment.

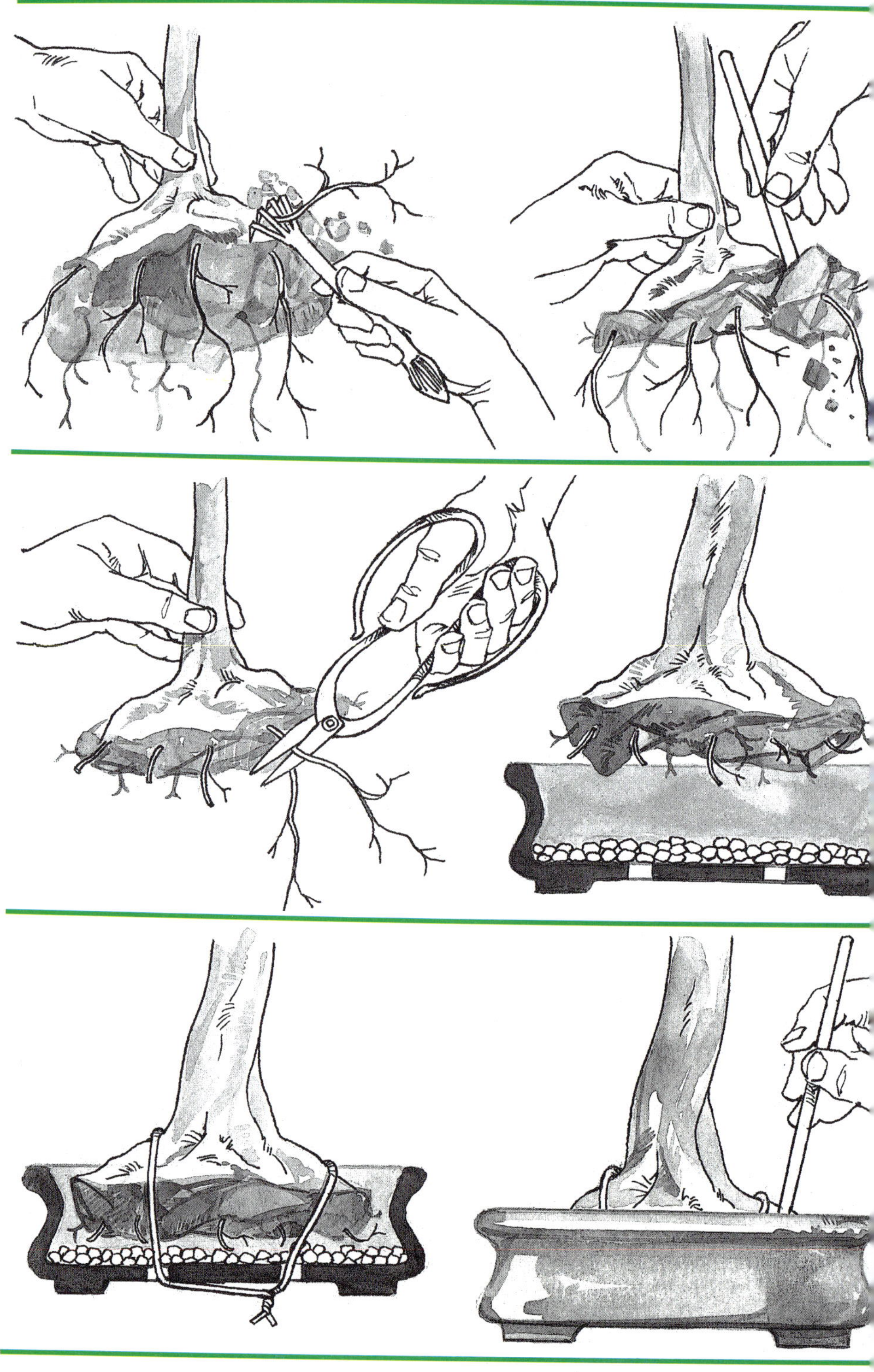

The first thing to do is to cut back all superfluous branches, with a view to reducing the surface area as much as possible allowing transpiration. The plant should be removed with its root system intact, and with a reasonable amount of its own soil, (normally a circle is drawn on the ground, following the circumference of the foliage, and the plant dug out accordingly, along this line).

Once extracted the plant must be wrapped in wet paper and in plenty of moss, then put in a plastic bag. As soon as you get home, plant it out carefully in a container, and place in an area which is very humid and protected from the sun. (To avoid excessive transpiration cover the plant with a perforated plastic bag for a period of several weeks.)

After about a year you can start with the bonsai treatment.

The best times for removing future bonsai from their natural environment are spring and autumn.

As well as wild plants you may wish to consider the multitude of potential bonsai subjects growing in your garden or in those of friends. Many of these plants can be bought in garden centers but not always at a very young stage, so you should have a good look round a garden to see what might be suitable.

Here then are a number of plants, starting with the English ivy, which, thanks to their shape, adapt particularly well to bonsai treatment.

Facing page: *Step-by-step method of repotting a bonsai.*
From the top, and from left to right: *Use the fork for freeing the roots, then with a small bamboo stick free the roots from the soil; cut the roots back accordingly; the bonsai is now ready for arranging in the container. Next anchor the plant to the container using the copper-coated aluminum wire, put in more soil pressing this down with the small bamboo stick.*

Ivy *(hedera helix)*

This is a typical climbing plant the main stem of which will cling to any kind of support, by means of small roots put out for this purpose. The leaves are evergreen, with a long stalk, and are coriaceous. They are bright green on the upper side and pale green underneath. The flowers are pentamerous in form, greenish-yellow in color but not particularly striking; they are arranged like umbrellas often bunched together at the end of the stem. The fruit is a roundish black berry containing two or three seeds.

Mimosa *(Acacia dealbata)*
This tree is common to the Mediterranean regions but is available in florists and garden centers elsewhere. The yellow flowers, which are tiny with restricted petals, are grouped together in globe-like clusters; they have many stamens with long slender filaments, giving the inflorescence a "flocky" appearance. Within the retinodes variety, which attains a height of five or six meters (16–20 feet) and a diameter of two or three meters (6–10 feet), flowering is continuous from spring to October. It is an ideal subject for grafting, and particularly suited to bonsai treatment. It needs plenty of light, and an airy location.

Bay laurel *(Laurus nobilis)*
This is an ornamental tree, grown for the beauty of its leafy branches, its elegant stance, and for its aromatic leaves. In its natural state, it prefers places sheltered from direct sunlight. As an evergreen shrub, its leaves are dark green in color, shiny, lanceolate, coriaceous, as well as scented. Both male and female plants produce minute flowers, greenish-yellow in color, which bloom in April. The female plants also produce blackish-purple berries.

Azalea *(Rhododendron)*
This is a family covering at least 500 species of greenhouse and hardy, evergreen and deciduous trees and shrubs. The Japanese azalea is commonly evergreen or semi-evergreen.

The leaves normally break out in an apex position, sometimes at the axis of the leaf, and can be either bell- or funnel-shaped and either flat or tubular. Originally from Asia, the popular deciduous outdoor variety grows well elsewhere in lime-free soil. The tortuous branches and the prostrate appearance of this plant, make it particularly suited to bonsai treatment.

Bamboo *(Bambus humilis)*
This is a woody plant which belongs to the large bamboo family. The multiplex species lends itself particularly well to bonsai cultivation. It needs plenty of light and water. Planting takes place in spring, in soil tending toward the humid. In April the rhizomes are divided and replanted immediately. The new leaves grow at the apex of the shoots, and in the case of bonsai treatment, they are to be clipped at the extremity before opening out.

Box *(Buxus sempervirens)*
From among the seventy evergreen and rustic Buxus varieties, generally only one of these is widely cultivated as a border and hedge plant, and trimmed into geometric shapes; this is the box tree, a species which can grow to a height of six meters (20 feet), reaching about two meters (6 feet) in diameter. It is a slow-growing tree, with a compact appearance, and has small, shiny dark-green oblate leaves. The flowers are insignificant, pale green in color with yellow anthers; they give off a perfume, and are grouped together in axillary clusters. This plant loves the sun but also areas of partial shade.

Bougainvillea (*Bougainvillea)*
These are climbing shrub-like plants, belonging to the Nyctaginate family. A dozen or so species are easily recognizable, the most famous being Bougainvillea *glabra* and Bougainvillea *spectabilis,* both originating in the virgin forests of Brazil. What are commonly but incorrectly thought of as the flowers are the vivid pink or crimson colored paper-like bracts which encircle the very insignificant flower groups.

Fig *(Ficus carica)*
Originally from the western part of Asia, this plant was introduced into Europe in ancient times. Normally the trunk is quite slender and the branches are delicate and irregular. The bark is quite thin, smooth, and ash-gray in color. The leaves, full and alternate, have between three and five lobes enlarged at their extremities and their margins are serrate. The upper side of the leaf is rough while the underside has a soft downiness. The flowers are unisexual and the fruit grows within the developing axis of the inflorescence.

Jasmin *(Jasminum officinalis)*
A shrub originating in south-west Asia, this plant is grown in Europe mainly for ornamental purposes. It has long slender green branches, which will always require some form of support. The leaves are basically rhomboid but also acute and oblong in shape and the leaf at the end of the stem is always longer than the others. The flowers, which are white and lightly perfumed, come into bloom in summer, presenting a gamopetalus corolla subdivided into five more or less convoluted lobes.

Juniper *(Juniperus)*
An evergreen, appearing either as a small tree or a shrub, the juniper belongs to the Cypress family and can be seen freely growing in woods on mountain-sides. Normally bushy and with creeping tendencies, this plant never reaches a great height. The bark is initially smooth and shiny, but then turns grayish-brown, and may peel off in long paper-like strips. The leaves, which are linear and needle-shaped, are dull grayish-green in color and arranged in verticils of three. The mock fruit (cones or berries) are roundish fleshy pseudo-berries created from the fusion of the floral bracts.

Hibiscus *(Hibiscus syriacus)*
This is a shrub belonging to the Malvaceae family. It includes about 200 varieties spread far and wide throughout the world, with a preference however for warm temperate zones. The flower itself has a small calyx, and the stamens have filaments joined together into a tube into which the style passes. Among the species cultivated as ornamental plants, the most common are the varieties *syriacus* and *rosa-sinensis*, the latter having a beautiful red flower.

Holm oak *(Quercus ilex)*
Originating in southern Europe and North Africa, this tree is one of the most common elements to be found in southern European scrubland. It can reach a height of 25 meters (82 feet) or so, but it is normally more evident in the form of a bush or small tree. The bark, which is gray and smooth when the tree is young, later breaks up into small plaque-like squares. The evergreen leaves are simple in style, thick and coriaceous with a small hairy stalk. The fruit is an elongated acorn, protected to about half-way by a cupola consisting of small triangular scales.

Mastic tree *(Pistacia lentiscus)*
This is a handsome bush or small tree, with pinnate leaves, shiny, hard, and green in color (although purple during the winter season), and which are also rich in tannin. A perfumed and viscose resin is extracted from this plant. It is one of the most common and abundant shrubs in the Mediterranean scrub areas, especially in the hotter regions of the south, accompanied in these areas by the wild olive. Its ashes, rich in potassium, make an excellent fertilizer. A very strong rustic plant, it can adapt to the most arid of climates.

Cultivation from seed

This is certainly an absorbing method, even though it will involve quite long timescales.

Cultivating an indoor bonsai from seed means, in the first place, growing a houseplant and then successfully transforming it into a bonsai.

From nurseries and garden-centers you can get hold of seeds from plants or fruit which are particularly suited to a future life in miniature. Exotic fruits are often used: from the avocado *(Persea americana)* to the pomegranate *(Punica granatum)*, from the pistachio *(Pistacia terebinthus)* to the citrus range. (From the various lemon species, for example, you can obtain *Averhoa carambola, Citrus lemon, Citrus aurantifolia,* and *Citrus sinensis.)* Persimmon *(Diospyros virginiana* and *D. Kaki)* and lychee *(Litchi chinensia)* are also excellent bonsai subjects.

Not all seeds, however, have the same germinating times, and many varieties need to be allowed to mature in fresh and airy surroundings. It is always a good idea to ask an expert gardener's advice, in order to weigh up which experiment to try out.

Many varieties of seed require some preliminary work on them before sowing can take place.

They need to be immersed in water for a period of 24 hours; during which time only those seeds which are fertile will absorb the water and sink to the bottom, so discard the others.

Immediately after this test you can proceed with the sowing.

The containers which you may use are many and varied (the important thing is that they should be at least 10 centimeters (4 inches) in height , and have adequate drainage holes).

The compost which is most recommended is the "weak" type, that is to say, not containing fertilizer and not sterilized, (normally you would use a mixture of peat and sand).

The container should be filled with the compost up to three centimeters (about 1 inch) from the rim; and once the soil has been leveled out, the seeds should be placed in (one by one in the case of larger-sized varieties, while very small ones may be sprinkled on), they should then be pressed gently into the soil (the larger seeds should be covered with a layer of already sieved compost), and then lightly watered.

It is very important that the seeds do not dry out. For this reason the container should be kept well out of the sun, and the soil should always be humid. The ideal ambient temperature range for this phase of the operation is 18–20°C (65–68°F).

Bonsai from seed.
Sow the seed after leveling out the compost; cover the seed with a layer of soil twice the seed diameter; gently firm down, then water and place in a sheltered position.

As soon as the first leaves appear, the baby plants may be transplanted one by one into small pots, or rearranged properly in the existing container. A month after this they can be fertilized (use a liquid organic fertilizer, but only half the dosage quantities as indicated in the instructions).

When the plants reach a height of 8–12 centimeters (3–4 inches), you can then begin to think in terms of what shape they are to take.

For example, cutting the principal shoot will induce the tree to develop lateral branches, which will then help to form the foliage of the bonsai.

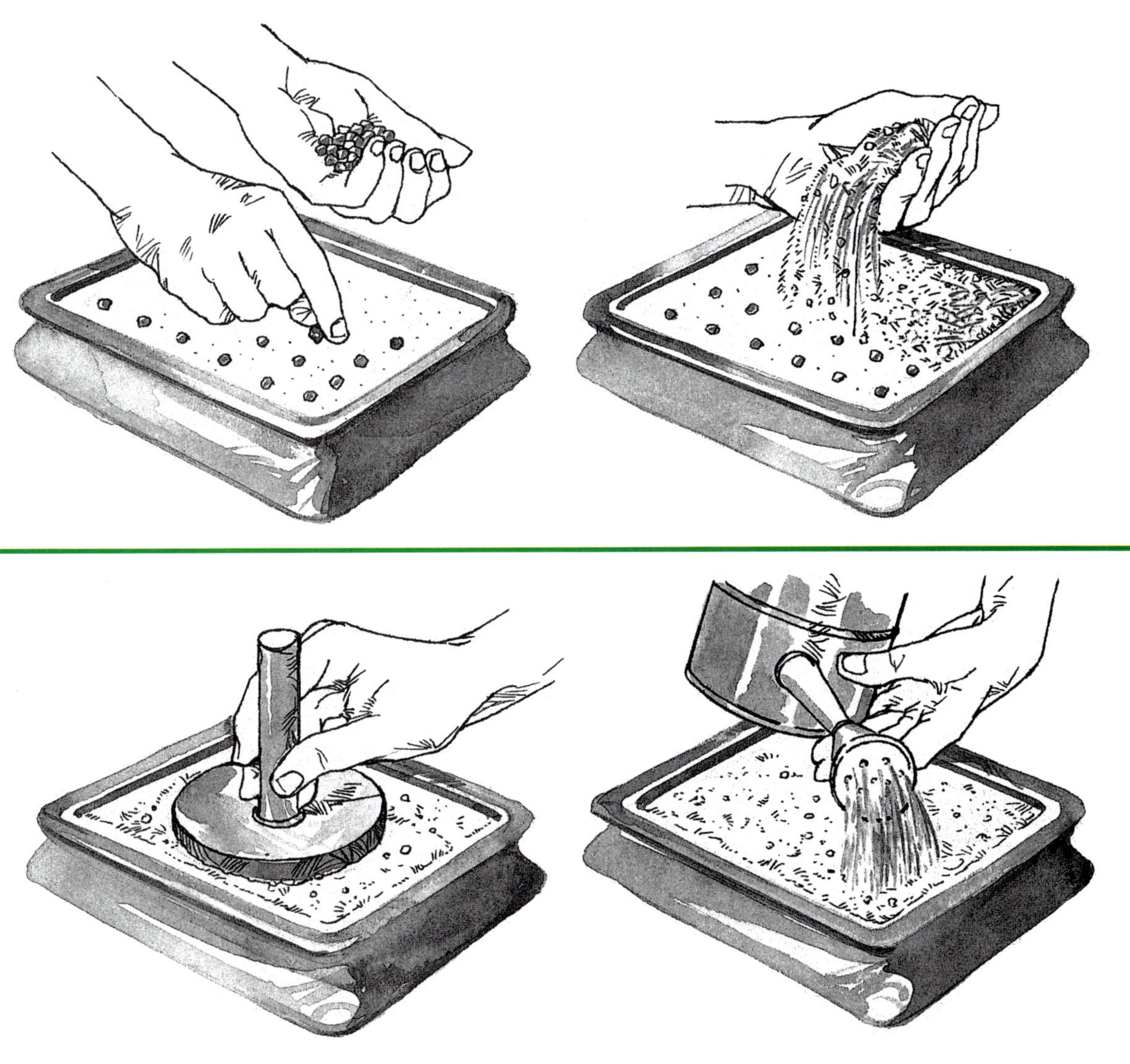

Propagation by cuttings

This system is highly practical and extensively used. It is carried out during one of the plant's resting periods and when both stems and small branches are completely mature. Once these have been cut from the plant, and either placed in the soil (or immersed in water), they then develop their own roots.

If the cutting is to have a proper root development, this will depend to a large extent on the care and attention with which the mother plant has been pruned the year previously, with this very purpose in mind. In fact this operation should be quite bold and rigorous, with a view to encouraging new shoots which, in turn, will have the right tendency for putting out roots.

Many houseplants can be reproduced by cuttings at any time during the year, though the best time is between April and June.

The branch to be pruned should be about 20 centimeters (8 inches) long, and should be cut back cleanly with a small sharp knife just below a leaf node. Planting in the soil should then take place only after all the leaves have been removed. To avoid loss of water, you should let only the bare minimum protrude from the soil so not to spoil the development of the buds. You can also encourage the growth of the plant by means of a rooting agent.

When this operation is complete, you should water plentifully and then cover the container with either a piece of transparent plastic or a

Bonsai produced from a cutting.
Cut off about 10–15 cm (4–6 inches) of mature wood; bury this in the soil up to the first bud; in a short time the plant will start to put out shoots.

large sheet of glass, the exception being well-fed plants whose shoots should be allowed to dry out at the base for about two weeks prior to transplanting into a dry compost. For such plant cuttings, before giving them their first watering, wait until they have put out their first tiny roots.

The most advisable compost for progation of cuttings is a mixture of sand and peat on a fifty-fifty basis; to be kept constantly humid. During the initial months the container should remain in surroundings where there is plenty of light, but not in the sun. Also ensure that cuttings from tropical plants are kept in warmer ambient conditions (18–24°C, 65–75°F) than those for hardier plants.

As soon as the young plants have put out their first tiny roots, you can then add a little fertilizer and then replace the cover on the container.

At that stage, as soon as the roots are ready, you can then go about transplanting into little pots containing compost suitable for indoor bonsai. Generally this should happen after a period of growth.

The cuttings of many houseplants can simply be immersed in a small glass receptacle of water to take root; make sure, however, that they are kept within their optimum temperature conditions, according to whether they are tropical or hardy varieties.

Once transplanted, the new plants can undergo their very first stages of bonsai treatment, which initially will consist of nipping back the new shoots from time to time, according to the eventual shape you want to achieve. As to fertilizer, you should apply this in lightly concentrated solutions, about a month after transplanting.

Bonsai produced from layering.
Cut into a point below the selected part, removing a strip of bark, and scrape clean with a knife; make up a ball of warm damp Sphagnum moss and fix it in place with a sheet of polythene. The layering is now ready to start producing roots.

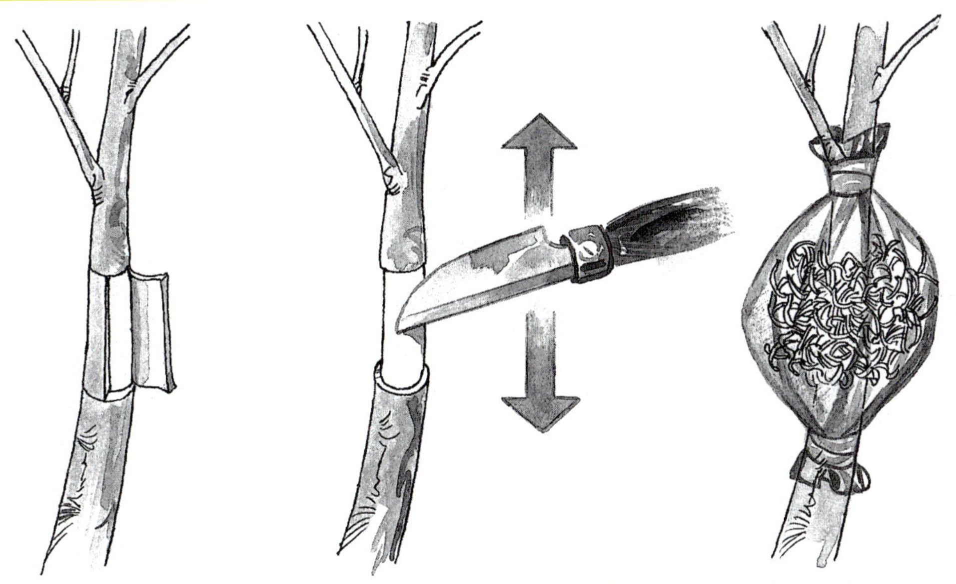

Propagation by layering

The advantage of this method is that the chosen section has grown a root system before being removed from the mother plant. It is best to use layering in the case of larger diameter shoots, where it might be difficult to reproduce them by the conventional cuttings method.

This technique also allows the bonsai grower to develop quite quickly new, already mature, trees. The best time to go about this operation is during a major growing phase, although reasonable results can also be obtained at any time throughout the year.

Firstly select your branch, remove the lateral shoots in one go, after having cut into the bark (in an upward direction for about two centimeters (1 inch) on either side of the area where you want the roots to form). Any bruising should then be treated with a root-hormone powder. You should then make up a ball of Sphagnum moss about 6–7 centimeters (2.5–3 inches) in diameter. Divide this in half, and spread both parts around the area of the stem which has already been prepared, kneading the moss in as compactly as possible. The whole lot is then kept tightly in place by means of a square sheet of black polythene, which is stuck to the stem with adhesive tape. You must also make sure that rain cannot penetrate and saturate the moss, so the two ends of the polythene sheet should be wrapped around spirally, using adhesive tape, in such a way that the tape also covers part of the stem to ensure a good seal.

To obtain an adequate root-formation from the layering process, you would normally need to wait one whole growing season but for houseplants, however, six to eight weeks should be enough. After this the branch should be self-supporting. It is then cut off below the point of the lower incision and planted in a pot or directly in a bonsai container, without removing the moss. As soon as the plant has taken root in the new container, you can start the bonsai treatment process.

Propagation by grafting

Various types of grafting. **From the top**, *split grafting; side-insertion grafting; direct T-form insertion; oval-inlay grafting.*

Grafting consists of bringing together two parts from different plants with a view to creating a new individual plant. In the case of bonsai cultivation, however, really successful grafting is very difficult to achieve so try and find an expert to help you.

One reason for grafting is the possibility of transferring the better qualities of one plant to another (referred to as transfer-grafting).

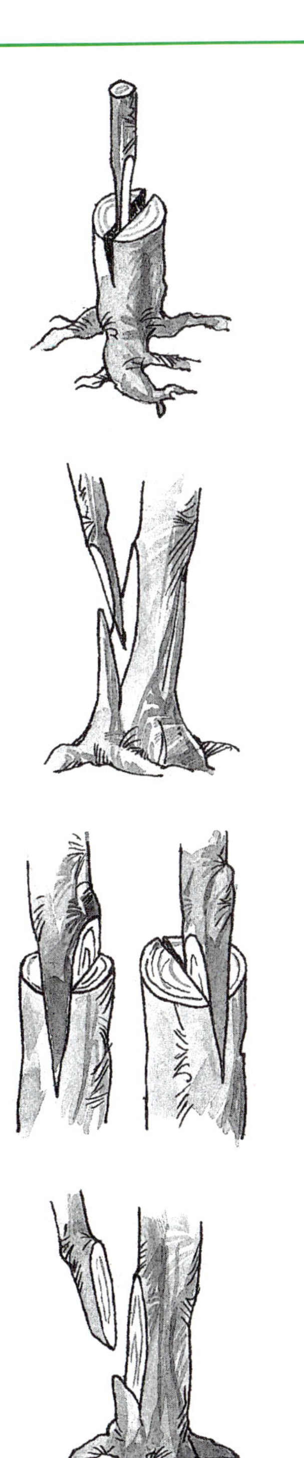

Various transfer-grafting techniques have been tried out involving fruit trees, with a view to improving other species of fruit plants. On the other hand, grafting can be used for decorative reasons and can also bring added benefit in terms of greater resistance to pests and diseases.

To achieve a perfect and natural union between two plants requires considerable preparation, a particular skill, a great deal of care and attention and some luck.

In terms of bonsai propagation the simpler methods of raising by seeding, cutting or layering can be highly satisfactory; particularly for the beginner.

Styles

When the young plant is ready for its initiation into bonsai, the first thing to do, after cutting out the larger, thicker roots, is to repot it in the right container. Only the capillaries should be left to stimulate the growth of the minor rootlets.

It is now time to consider the external shape of the plant. In order to qualify for the name, a bonsai must be shaped like a natural tree – in miniature. Foliage, trunk, branches, leaves and flowers, must retain pleasing and balanced proportions.

For this reason the young tree should be kept under constant observation, pruned, trimmed, and in some instances "assisted" using the wiring technique. Indoor bonsai, in particular, which continue growing throughout the year, require constant uninterrupted attention.

The bonsai grower's first priority, therefore, is to decide on the shape which will best suit the plant always bearing in mind what it would look like as a fully grown plant in its natural habitat.

Firstly the plant should be very carefully examined with a view to understanding its internal structure and then, by means of the bonsai process, the grower should set about interpreting the plant to its best possible advantage.

All classical bonsai shapes reflect careful observation of natural phenomena, which have enabled bonsai artists to create the right proportions and sizes.

If you are thinking about entering your bonsai trees for exhibitions in the future, it is essential that you know the traditional styles of bonsai so that your compositions are "judged" by fellow enthusiasts within their correct classifications. The following are the principal classical bonsai styles developed over the years.

Upright style *(chokkan)*

The branches grow symmetrically and horizontally around an upright straight trunk. The first branch up from the bottom is the longest, and in proportion must grow to an equivalent of a third of the total height of the tree. As they ascend the branches taper assuming a cone-like form. It is also possible to have a "free" form, whereby the trunk grows in curves which become sharper nearer the foliage, while the branches grow only on the outside edge of the curves.

Curved trunk style *(moyogi)*

In this case the plant retains a very natural appearance, thanks to the curving nature of the trunk. The branches get smaller in size toward the top, growing also on the outside edge of the curves.

Leaning trunk style *(shakan)*

The trunk leans to one side; the branches are positioned horizontally, shooting out in all directions. The surface roots are clearly visible on the side opposite to "the lean".

Windswept style ***(fukinagashi)***

This differs from the previous style in that the branches grow on one side of the trunk only (the way the tree is leaning). This gives the impression of the wind blowing continually from one direction.

Broom style ***(hokidachi)***

So called because of its similarity in appearance to an upturned broom. Its spread of branches, in the shape of a fan, may occupy nearly half the total height of the tree. The trunk is upright.

Cascade style ***(kengai)***

Just as if they are bursting out of a rock, the branches grow out over the edge of the container and lean downward. Make sure that the container you choose for this style is high enough to show off the cascade effect to best advantage.

Multiple trunk style ***(kabudaki)***

Trunks are allowed to grow from a single root which has put out several shoots. The result of this is a little group of trees. Generally they should make up an odd number but if only two trunks appear, they should be different sizes.

Raft style ***(ikadabuchi)***

This style creates the effect of a fallen trunk, which has put out roots downward, and branches upward. The final impression, which is quite original, is one of a group of individual plants all springing from a horizontal trunk.

Woodland ***(yose-ue)***

This is the most fascinating of all the bonsai styles. In a single container a number of individual plants of the same species are laid out in a correctly proportioned manner. An important rule of this style is that all the plant examples be of differing ages and sizes. The end-result should seek to obey the rules of proportion and harmony.

Twisted trunk style
The trunk diminishes in size toward the top and gives the appearance of twisting in upon itself; the branches break out in all directions. The overall aspect is similar to ***chokkan***.

"Literati" style *(bunjingi)*
This style is characterized principally by the branches growing exclusively at the apex of the plant. The bare trunk may also be allowed to lean more or less in one direction. The effect can be of either standing on rock, in woodland style, blown by the wind, or standing erect. The important thing is that the plant should express its own particular internal balance, and the major factor here is the bearing of the trunk.

On rock *(ishitsuki)*
A piece of rock is placed appropriately in the container, to be embraced eventually by the roots of the bonsai. These, however, sink into the soil below. Once the little tree starts growing and putting out roots into the small cavities in the rock, you then have your so-called "rock-planting".

Containers

A bonsai cannot be called as such, unless, in the interests of visual form, its container is also taken into account. Containers come in all shapes, sizes, and colors: tall or flat, round or rectangular, glazed, and sometimes are valuable antiques. Employing skill and good taste, the enthusiast must choose whatever is going to suit the particular species best, being mindful also of its future shape.

Ceramic art and production developed in the Far East at the same time that the art of bonsai began to spread. In Japan, for example, six types of pottery are recognized, with over a thousand years of history. The most ancient is that of *Tokoname;* an example of an art-form without equal anywhere in the world.

長春

The container in which the bonsai grows and develops will complete an overall well-proportioned display; and it is up to the grower's own artistic sense to make sure the choice is right. Every bonsai style has its preferred container format: styles which contain erect plants call for relatively shallow vessels, while cascade styles need taller, narrower ones. Oval-shaped pots are particularly suited to groups of trees.

The height of the container is also very important, but not simply esthetically; it should also suit the daily growing conditions of the plant.

The color of the container must also harmonize with those of the leaves and the flowers. Its decoration can involve a braid pattern, single or double; or a cornice plain or patterned. The edges also can be plain, both outside and in, or plate-shaped. Feet are also very important in that they allow air to circulate underneath the container. They can be flattish, cat's-paw- or cloud-shaped.

In China, the center of unglazed pottery was the prefectural district of Yi Xing, in the province of Yang Su, where in the manufacturing process the pots were fired in long kilns. It has always been from the Far East that we have imported the secrets of how to obtain red, white, black and purple earthenware. Even today, the Japanese and Chinese specialists are at the forefront in the creation of pieces both highly valuable and innovative in style.

You will find a large variety of vessels and containers to choose from in specialist bonsai suppliers but when making your choice you should always try to remember the following.

- The length of the container in general should be equivalent to two-thirds of the height of the trunk; and its height should not be less than the thickness of the trunk.

- Upright plants are better suited to the flatter type of container, while cascading plants prefer taller vessels.

- You should always keep in mind what color the leaves and flowers are going to be. For example, flowering plants with light-colored foliage look at their best in containers with a dark-colored glaze.

Occasional tables for displaying bonsai.

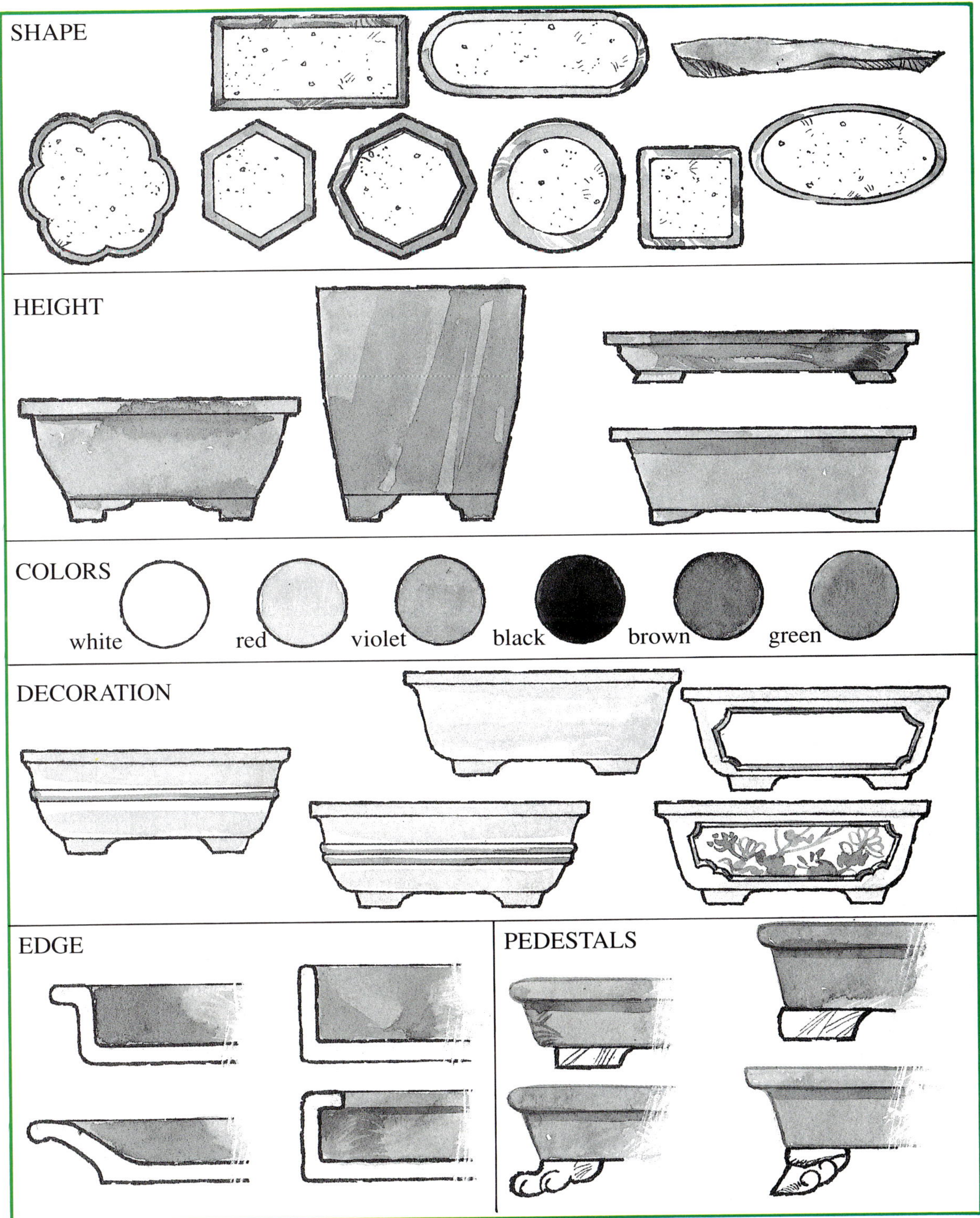
SHAPE
HEIGHT
COLORS
white
red
violet
black
brown
green
DECORATION
EDGE
PEDESTALS

Indoor Bonsai Compositions

Having considered the creation and the nurturing of the single bonsai plant, we can now see how the art and experience of many years can merge to create really authentic group compositions. These also make ideal indoor decoration.

These ideas and concepts are for the amateur who already has some experience and who can unite good taste and creative passion with a certain technical ability, bringing together forms and shapes as diverse as the weeping willow, the umbrella, the cone, the sphere and so on.

Forest-group

To create the traditional forest-group you need at least five trees and, in any event, you should always have an odd number. The plants should then be sub-divided into two groups, according to size (or shape) and height.

You should choose a very shallow container, either oval or rectangular in shape. The trees should be of the same species, to facilitate care and maintenance but they should all differ in size and age.

The largest and strongest tree will assume the role of the "main" tree, and will be planted first, possibly slightly off-center, in relation to the shape of the container. The other specimens will be arranged around this one, either singly, or in little groups.

Generally those with the more developed branches will be planted round the edge, while the smaller specimens will stay inside the group.

The fig variety *Ficus benjamina* and the elm are all highly suitable for this type of composition.

A forest of exceptionally large pine trees (at least two by three meters in area, about six by nine feet) has been created inside an apartment. To achieve this however, you would need a number of technical and architectural tricks up your sleeve, such as the right lighting and proper ventilation. The whole composition was contained within a box arrangement made of glass and wood with an open top; the end result was indeed spectacular.

A final piece of advice: forest-group bonsai need precisely the same care and attention as any other indoor bonsai. Repotting should normally take place every two years. The composition can look more natural if enhanced with small pieces of fern, or vegetation typical of the undergrowth.

Facing page: **above:** *conifer plants selected to create a forest-group.* **Below:** *a selection of fig plants planted as a forest-group.*

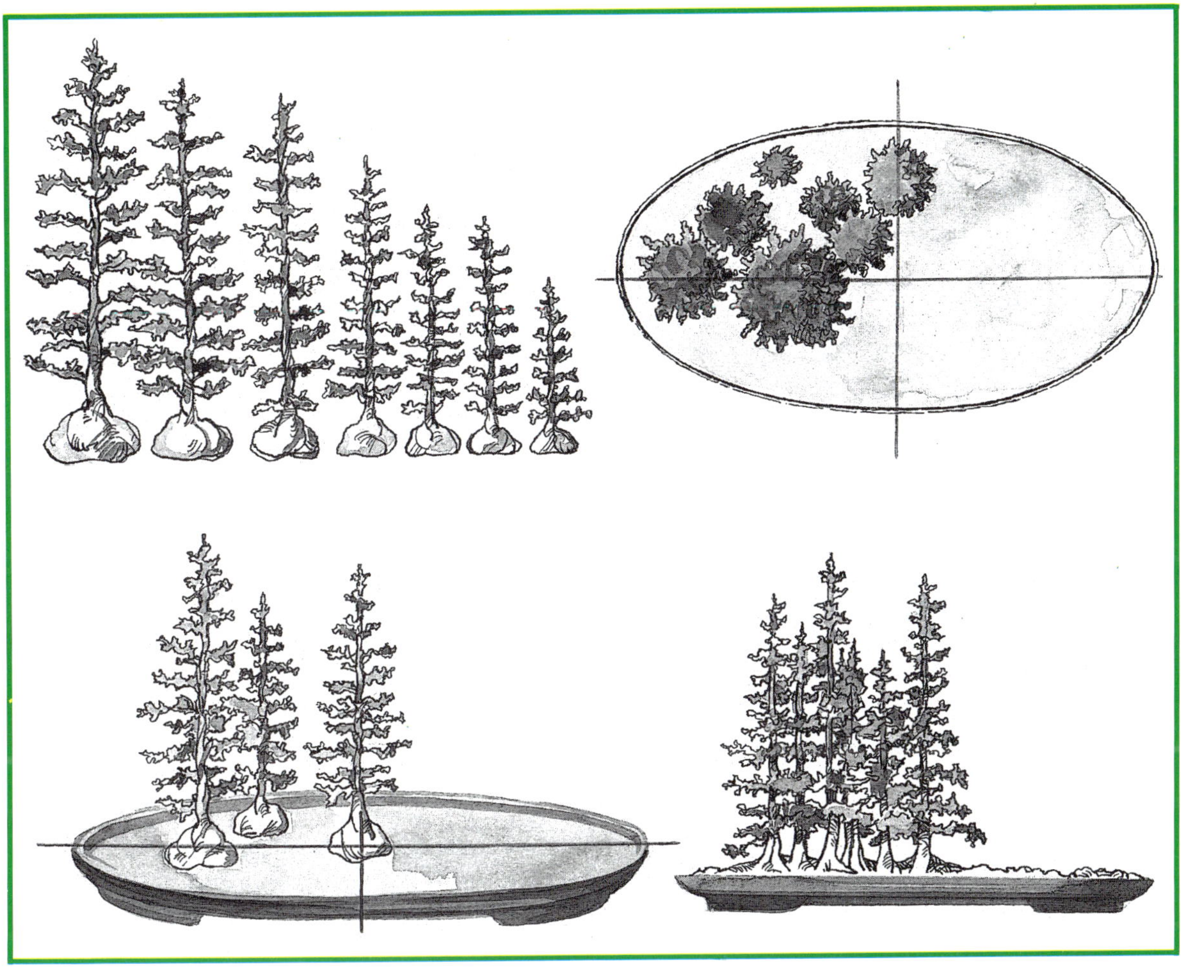

Once the young plants have been selected for the creation of the fig tree forest-group, note in the photographs below the step-by-step positioning of the individual specimens in a container specially chosen for this type of composition.

Facing page, *the completed group. Note that the intermediate-sized trees have been placed each side of the main tree.*

Composition on rock

For this type of composition plants with long strong roots are necessary, such as many of the fig varieties, the schefflara, and the tea-plant.

The roots must grip the rock, on which the plant has been fixed, and carry on growing downward until they reach the soil. To achieve this you will need a special hormone rooting preparation for stimulating the root-growth.

In this case, fill a plastic container with a mixture of 20 percent peat and 80 percent sand (commercially available bonsai compost is also suitable, provided it is of a large grading). The container should be of a similar height to that of the sample of rock chosen for this composition, and it should also have drainage holes.

Plant the young tree in the container. Every six to eight weeks reduce the height of the container (by cutting off a piece of the edge), and remove the excess soil. By this means, you will be freeing an ever lengthening section of the root and, at the same time, the part which remains buried will be encouraged to grow more quickly and more vigorously.

When the greater part of the root is thus free, the tree is ready for transplanting onto the rock. The rock itself, can be large, small, or of any shape or color.

In this type of bonsai there are no limitations, except those of the creative imagination of the enthusiast and of his or her ability to observe the thousands of forms and facets of nature.

Sometimes, the rock may be placed within the plastic container so that the roots grow over the surface of the rock from the start, and have a good grip well before the plant is transferred into its bonsai display container. Generally however, it will require a little care and attention to arrange the roots over your chosen piece of rock as they grow down.

Superb effects can be achieved with tropical varieties which have airborne roots.

After successful planting upon the rock, the bonsai should be allowed to remain resting for about two months. During this time it should be kept well out of the sun, and sprayed frequently.

Once this period is over, you should give it a good fertilizing and apply all the normal care and attention you would give to any indoor bonsai.

Another method of bonsai rock-composition consists of growing the tree within a cavity or within a fissure in the rock face, though this spot must be prepared beforehand with a layer of compost (peat and clay on a fifty-fifty basis).

A composition involving a number of plants growing on rock: Chamaecyparis, Cryptomeria japonica, Carpinus coreana, Azalea japonica.

The tree may be fixed to the rock by means of double-sided tape and the roots should be covered with warm damp compost. In order to create an undergrowth, you should select small plants which will grow quickly and protect the soil from being loosened during watering. For indoor purposes, evergreen creepers are highly suitable.

As these rock-based landscapes are built on very little soil, they require frequent watering and careful fertilizing. You should also be constantly checking the level of the compost and adding to it if necessary.

Small forest-group of Jaikei elm

Facing page:
Detail of the same Jaikei elm *forest-group, in which a small lake is visible, on the shore of which two Chinamen are seated, drinking tea.*

Saikei

The term *saikei* means the art of creating a miniature landscape. This too is a form of bonsai, which goes back to the tradition of the most celebrated Japanese gardens, even though the origins of this type of composition are to be found in China.

Saikei can be found with miniature statues, tiny houses, and other landscape items, contained within them. However, in its "purest" form, this type of bonsai calls exclusively for natural items, such as trees, soil, rock, and sand.

In order to create a bonsai landscape, you would go about it in exactly the same way as if preparing a forest-group. Plants of the same species are generally chosen, but of different ages and sizes, (even though they should all be relatively young). The trees should then be introduced into the landscape itself.

At this point the imagination of the bonsai enthusiast comes into play; who, through an inspired choice of miniature rocks and stones, should open up the widest horizons.

It is also a question of experimenting with sizes and proportions, colors and perspectives, to create a scene that is both remarkable and individual. For additional resources, the bonsai enthusiast can draw on the variety of undergrowth plants, invaluable for their ability to evoke atmosphere.

Note: Always use a shallow container, either oval or rectangular in shape, and the same precautions which you took for forest planting also apply for *saikei.* After planting, allow the trees to rest for several weeks. During this time do not fertilize, keep them out of strong sunlight but in good light conditions.

Bonkei

The use of stones and pebbles in a *saikei* composition are also part of another artistic technique from the Far East; that of *bonkei.*

Both in fact originate in Zen philosophy, introduced into Japan from China in the late twelfth century. The school of Zen Buddhism teaches that contemplation of one's essential nature to the exclusion of all else is the single way to achieve complete and pure enlightenment. Chinese Zen had developed within the hardship of monastic life and early paintings depicted monks in contemplation amid an austere mountainous landscape of rocks, sparsely leaved shrubs, and coniferous trees.

There are five "keys" available to the observer; the rock can be seen as a mountain, as an abstract representation of an animal, as a stylized figure; it can be chosen for its colors or for the imaginary flowers to be seen growing on its surface.

As in the case of the bonsai, it is essential too that the *bonkei* be placed in the appropriate container, which will serve to heighten the "reading" of the subject.

The only human participation which is allowed in *bonkei,* is the arrangement of the container, in which case the base of the selected stone may be cut and shaped accordingly. The natural growth cannot be tampered with in any other way, and it is essential when displayed, that the *bonkei* succeeds in showing off to best advantage its sides and its most notable features. Characteristically these compositions give out a feeling of peace and tranquillity, while still retaining their own essential vitality, itself a reflection of human thought.

A group of Criptomeria japonica *growing on rock*

Mini-bonsai

Plant miniaturization has gone to extremes in the last few years, giving rise to so-called mini-bonsai. These plants are often not more than 8–15 centimeters high (3–6 inches) and grown in containers often no bigger than a thimble.

These tiny trees can quite easily be reared from seed, or obtained from a cutting. Once you have decided upon the appropriate shape, you should remove all the new shoots with a pair of clippers, leaving only one or two leaves.

The mini-bonsai should be repotted annually and a third of its roots cut off.

Since only a little soil is available to the mini-bonsai, they have to receive the most meticulous care and attention. During the growing period, they should be fertilized once a week with a liquid feed. They should be watered at least once a day, (ideally they should be immersed completely in water) and then placed on a tray specially prepared with a granulate or with warm damp sand. Apart from these precautions, the general rules for any indoor bonsai will also apply.

Mini-bonsai are enchanting plants and are well suited for indoor decoration, particularly when arranged in groups.

Rose mignon *bonsai*
(11 years old)

Azalea (Rhododendron)
growing on rock
(23 years old)

Sage (Salvia Officinalis)
(6 years old)

Hosta (H. undulata)
Bailey (9 years old)

Useful information

As in the case of all houseplants, bonsai also require looking after whenever you are away from home.

One solution could be to leave the plant in the hands of a nursery or, alternatively, ask a relative or friend to help you out.

In this case however you should give precise instructions to your temporary assistant, in case your bonsai suffers from an excess of "zeal" on his or her part.

If you are away for a short period (not more than six days), the bonsai may be left untended, provided it has been sufficiently well watered beforehand, that is to say, immersed together with its container in a bowl filled with well-soaked peat. The plant should be left in an area which is not too hot and well away from strong sunlight. You can also create a mini-greenhouse effect around your bonsai, by using a transparent plastic bag to prevent the water from evaporating.

If you are going to be away for some time however, it might be an idea to place a wedge of terracotta in the soil, connected by a tube to a container full of water. You can also get the same result by running a length of wool thread down to the soil from a bucket of water placed at a higher level. The water seeps slowly down the thread, until eventually it reaches the plant.

Both these methods need checking periodically to ensure that all is going well; that obstructions are not getting in the way of the terracotta wedge, and that the wool thread has not shifted from its original position. Also you should ensure that during your absence the plant does not suffer from lack of light, or any sudden changes in temperature.

Whenever you buy a bonsai, you should have in mind several tricks of the trade, which you will find invaluable in maintaining and caring for your plant.

Firstly you should check the quality and the general state of health of the root system. This must be firm and well developed. To be sure of this, just take the plant out of the pot and check to see if the soil block is compact and if the tiniest of the rootlets are visible on the outside (they should be white during the growth phase).

The retailer may often try to make out that the plant is older than it really is but, when you make your purchase, you must ensure that the specimen has the correct proportions and is in good health. Only if the plant is especially old, and it is this fact alone which is determining its market value, should you be on the look-out for additional information, or even asking for the opinion of an expert.

Generally speaking, in order to guide your choice, good taste is enough, together with an expert eye, gained from regularly reading trade literature and from frequent attendance at bonsai shows and exhibitions.

Every good bonsai must comply with the following six basic requirements:

- it must have a healthy appearance
- its trunk must be well-proportioned, tapering toward the top
- its branches must be more delicate toward the outside of the plant
- its leaves must be healthy and of the right shape and proportions
- its roots must develop in an orderly fashion, though being allowed a modicum of freedom

Bonsai clubs are to be found in many towns and cities where beginners can receive much valuable advice and tuition on bonsai practice from experienced enthusiasts. These clubs often put on excellent courses dealing with both theory and technique, in addition to refresher courses given by famous oriental experts.

These clubs are also on hand at shows and exhibitions, and many publish useful material. Joining a bonsai club, therefore, means meeting friends of a similar interest, with whom you may try out ideas and innovations, in a sphere of activity where experience and imagination know no limits.

Indoor Bonsai

Pistachio (Pistacia chinensis) *approximately 200 years old*

Azalea

(Rhododendron)

General characteristics A shrub with small, semi-evergreen leaves and marvellous flowers in a wide variety of colors, innumerable combinations and degrees of shading.

Recommended ambient conditions In summer, place in an area of half light / half shade which is lightly ventilated. In winter, keep in a light yet sheltered location, in a temperature of 2–8°C (35–46F).

Watering Plentiful throughout the year, maintaining constant humidity. Spray the leaves when the plant is not in flower. Use soft or rain water. Ensure the water does not become stagnant.

Fertilizing From June to August with a slow-yielding organic fertilizer.

Repotting Every two to three years after flowering, together with pruning the aerial roots and cutting back the main roots.

Soil 100% special azalea soil (or ericaceous compost), alternatively 40% peat, 40% azalea soil, 20% river sand. Ensure drainage is effective at all times.

Wiring In spring or October / early November; be careful, however, since the young branches are very fragile.

Propagation From seed, which is collected in May and planted at the same time in a substrate of peat and sand in equal measure; this to be kept humid. By cuttings, taken in June, for planting under glass in a compost of 50% peat and 50% sand. By layering also, to be carried out at end June / early July, to be separated in September/October of the following year.

Flowering From April onward.

Azalea (Rhododendron lateritum) *18 years old*

Azalea (Rhododendron) *55 years old*

Azalea japonica *35 years old*

Bamboo

(Bambusa humilis)

General characteristics	A graceful Japanese dwarf variety, with stems showing green internodes, the upper ones being frosty-white in color. Underneath the nodes reveal considerable humidity in winter. This plant grows best in partial shade and dislikes direct sunlight.
Recommended ambient conditions	In winter, keep indoors in a bright location, with a temperature 14–18°C (57–65°F). Place outside from May to September in a shady area.
Watering	This should be plentiful throughout the entire year; maintaining a constant level of humidity. When inside spray every day.
Fertilizing	Slow-yielding organic fertilizer in spring and September/October.
Repotting	For young plants, every year in spring; every two years for older plants.
Soil	40% akadama earth in medium-sized granules, 40% river sand, 20% soil. Watch the drainage carefully.
Pruning	Continual clipping of the terminals, before these open out. This will keep the bonsai compact.
Wiring	Not necessary.
Propagation	This plant is propagated by dividing the foot before the growth phase resumes; however, any such removals should be ruthless, if not, new growth will tend to be very slow.

Bamboo (Bambusa humilis)

Bougainvillea

(Bougainvillea glabra)

General characteristics A native of the Brazilian rain-forests, with small flowers, oval bracts which are also reticulate, and possessing a sensational range of color shades, from pinkish crimson to pink-lilac, which produce splendid long-lasting blooms. From June to September, it has a shrub-like appearance, and can grow to a height of 6–9 meters (19–30 feet). The branches are slightly thorny.

Recommended ambient conditions Indoors, wherever there is plenty of bright light and a temperature of 12–17°C (53–62°F). From May to September, keep in a sunny location.

Watering Plentiful in summer but not excessively for fear of losing the leaves. In winter water carefully.

Fertilizing Apply an organic slow-yielding fertilizer right up to the beginning of summer. Repeat in September.

Repotting Every 2–3 years in spring, accompanied by root-pruning.

Soil 70% graded peat, 30% light colored peat. Watch the drainage carefully.

Pruning Right up to the first days of summer. When the flowering is over, prune again to continue reshaping the tree.

Propagation By means of woody and partially woody cuttings in spring, in a compost consisting of 70% sand and 30% peat, preferably with warm drainage and in generally humid conditions. In winter keep sheltered, but in an area where there is plenty of light.

Flowering From June to September.

Bougainvillea (Bougainvillea variegata) *65 years old*

Box

(Buxus harlandii)

General characteristics Indigenous to the Far East and to the shores of the Mediterranean, this is a decorative evergreen shrub with numerous branches. The Harland variety can grow to a height of 12–13 meters (40–43 feet).

Recommended ambient conditions Should be placed in front of a window which does not have a southerly exposure. From May to September place outdoors in half-light.

Watering Soak plentifully during the summer. In winter, take action appropriate to ambient conditions.

Fertilizing During winter, if the plant is in a fresh and airy location, fertilizing is not necessary. If, however, the area is somewhat warm, add fertilizer every six weeks. From April to October fertilize every three weeks.

Repotting To be undertaken preferably between April and October, accompanied by root-pruning.

Soil 60% akadama earth in medium-sized granules, 30% light colored peat, 10% sand.

Pruning Possible right up to the end of August. After flowering, cut off completely the flowering shoots.

Wiring Possible at any time throughout the year.

Propagation By cuttings of mature wood. By layering, working only, however, on branches which have become woody.

Flowering November, December, January.

Box (Buxus Harlandii) *approximately 19 years old*

Calamondin
(Calamondin Orange)

(Citrus Mitis)

General characteristics Indigenous to the Philippines, this plant reaches a height of 3–4 meters (10–13 feet), with lanceolate leaves, darkish in color. The flowers form groups of three or four together, and the round-shaped fruit, yellowish-orange in color, have an acid pulp.

Recommended ambient conditions Ideally in a fresh well ventilated location with plenty of bright light. In summer it can tolerate temperatures of 7–12°C (44–53°F). Place outdoors from March to the end of October.

Watering Water plentifully during the summer period, and in winter avoid any excesses of humidity.

Fertilizing Apply only after flowering, and then with an organic product. Do not fertilize during hot periods.

Repotting Every two to three years, after collecting the fruit.

Soil 40% light colored peat, 40% soil, 20% graded akadama earth.

Pruning After flowering, carry out a general maintenance pruning from late spring until September/October, watching out for the fruit, which will already be present on the branches.

Wiring Wiring of the branches can be carried out from spring until the end of summer.

Propagation From seed, in March, in a possible temperature of 13–16°C (55–60°F).

Flowering Late summer.

Fruit-bearing August-September.

Calamondin (Citrus mitis) *9 years old*

Camellia

(Camellia japonica)

General characteristics This species can be either arboreal or shrub-like. When it reaches a height of 6–7 meters ((20–22 feet) it assumes the form of a bush with plenty of branches. At 12–15 meters (40–50 feet) it has the appearance of a normal tree. The leaves are ovate-elliptical in shape, the wood is compact and extremely hard, trunk or bark are smooth. The leaves are semi-evergreen and the flowers grow singly.

Recommended ambient conditions In winter, place in a fresh and airy location with plenty of bright light, in temperature conditions ranging from 4 to 13°C (39–55°F). Place outdoors but sheltered from the sun, from March to September. Ensure a proper flow of fresh air.

Watering Water plentifully during the summer season, maintaining average humidity. In winter avoid excesses of humidity, which will cause the leaves to turn yellow and to fall.

Fertilizing After flowering and pruning, with plenty of organic fertilizer. Do not fertilize during periods of hot weather, or in winter.

Repotting Every two to three years, after flowering, plus root-pruning.

Soil 40% peat, 40% ericaceous compost, 10% sand, 10% clay.

Pruning This plant tolerates pruning very well; clip very carefully leaving three shoots. The most important pruning is the one carried out after flowering. No pruning after June.

Wiring This can be done throughout the whole year. At the beginning of spring, be particularly cautious. Wire any new shoots only after these have become woody.

Propagation By grafting preferably in spring. By semi-ripe cuttings in spring, by woody cuttings in September/October. Also from seed.

Flowering End of February, March.

Fruit-bearing End of July, August.

Camellia
(Camellia japonica)
16 years old

Chinese Pistachio

(Pistacia chinensis)

General characteristics A tree variety indigenous to China, with extraordinary pointed light-green leaves and a distinctive gray trunk. It can grow to a height of 7–9 meters (23–30 feet).

Recommended ambient conditions Indoors in a situation with plenty of light, and a temperature of 14–19°C (57–66°F). Keep outdoors from May to September in partial shade.

Watering Plentifully all year round but allowing the soil to dry out slightly before each new watering. When indoors spray daily.

Fertilizing From May to September, slow-yielding organic fertilizer. In winter twice only.

Repotting Every two to three years, in early spring, plus root-pruning.

Soil 40% peat, 30% soil, 20% graded earth, 10% sand. Ensure proper drainage.

Pruning Throughout the year, making sure, however, to leave three to four leaves remaining on the shoots to be pruned.

Wiring Throughout the year but carefully.

Propagation From seed.

Fruit-bearing Late summer.

Chinese pistachio (Pistacia chinensis) *42 years old.*

Chrysanthemum

(Chrysanthemum)

General characteristics Indigenous to China, this is a perennial plant which blooms in summer and grows easily, reaching a height of 65–70 centimeters (25–27 inches). The flowers are generally 3–5 centimeters (1–2 inches) in diameter and appear on branch-like stems between summer and September/October. The lobate leaves are mid-green in color. It is a highly resistant plant, not easily prone to pests and diseases. More than 200 species have been recorded; herbaceous and part-shrubby, annuals, perennials, rustic and semi-rustic.

Recommended ambient conditions It dislikes the cold, and much prefers situations with plenty of sun.

Watering Plentiful during the summer.

Fertilizing Throughout the year, except during flowering.

Repotting Every two to three years, together with pruning a third of the roots.

Soil 90% graded earth, 10% compost.

Pruning After flowering.

Wiring Not necessary.

Propagation By cuttings, or from seed.

Flowering Late summer.

Korean Chrysanthemum

Common Jasmine Orange

(Murraya paniculata)

General characteristics A native of tropical and sub-tropical Asia, it is dispersed throughout Indonesia and Malaysia. It possesses large, single, highly perfumed white flowers; and has oblong or ovoid red berries. It has a hard, clear and smooth trunk, from which items such as walking sticks are made and cosmetic oils obtained.

Recommended ambient conditions When indoors, keep in an area with plenty of light, in a temperature of 10–20°C (50–68°F) but out of direct sunlight. From May to September keep outdoors in a shady area.

Watering Consistently throughout the entire year, at the same time keeping the soil fresh and not allowing the water to become stagnant.

Fertilizing In spring and summer with a slow-yielding, organic fertilizer, but avoiding fertilizing when fruit and flowers are in evidence. Fertilize twice in winter.

Repotting In spring (April–May), every two or three years, together with root-pruning.

Soil Prefers light soil composts: 40% ericaceous compost, 40% peat, 10% sand, 10% akadama.

Pruning All the year round for the branches. The longer shoots should be cut back to two or three leaves during the growing period.

Wiring All year round.

Propagation By means of cuttings, using a woody, leafy branch planted in sandy compost under a bell-shaped glass jar, with the base soil slightly warm in order to encourage rooting.

Flowering Late August to September.

Fruit-bearing October–November.

Common Jasmine Orange (Murraya paniculata) *22 years old.*

Common Jasmine Orange

Cork Oak

(Quercus suber)

General characteristics This most ancient of varieties, indigenous to the Iberian peninsula, Sardinia and Corsica, is distinguished by its reddish-colored trunk, which twists and turns with the passage of time, creating a cracked cork-like bark. It is an evergreen, and normally attains a height of 10 meters (32 feet) but in certain circumstances can even reach 20 to 25 meters (65–82 feet), together with a trunk-diameter of over a meter (3 feet).

Recommended ambient conditions From May to the end of October keep outdoors in a sunny position. This plant begins to suffer at temperatures below 5°C (41°F).

Watering Regular, but moderate in winter.

Fertilizing Slow-yielding organic fertilizer in spring and September/October.

Repotting Every two to three years in spring, accompanied by a light pruning. Proceed with care.

Soil 60% graded acidic earth, 20% light-colored peat, 20% river-sand. Must be kept well drained.

Pruning In late spring. Clipping, however, all year round.

Wiring Early summer.

Propagation From seed, or by layering, at the beginning of summer.

Cork oak (Quercus suber) *35 years old.*

Elaeagnus

(Elaeagnus)

General characteristics A shrub-like variety indigenous to Asia. It can, however, reach a height of 7–8 meters (23–26 feet), and has semi-evergreen leaves. It also produces a small white axillary flower with a red berry. The trunk is robust, and the branch-network is dense, but slightly thorny. Suitable for indoor cultivation.

Recommended ambient conditions Indoors, in a bright and airy location, with a temperature between 13 and 18°C (55–65F). From May to September outdoors in partial shade.

Watering Plentiful, keeping the soil slightly humid. When indoors, spray every day.

Fertilizing From May to September with a slow-yielding organic fertilizer. Do not fertilize in winter.

Repotting Every two to three years in spring, together with root-pruning.

Soil 50% compost, 20% graded akadama, 20% peat, 10% river sand.

Pruning Spring and the beginning of summer.

Wiring Any time during the year, but only on woody plants.

Propagation From seed, or by cuttings under cold glass conditions, to be taken in August either from young partially woody branches, or from root suckers to be separated in spring.

Flowering Late summer.

Fruit-bearing End September to October.

Elm (Chinese Elm)

(Ulmus parvifolia)

General characteristics A very interesting tree, which in China and Japan can reach a height of 18–20 meters (60–65 feet). It features obovate-shaped and serrated-edged leaves which are semi-evergreen, branches which are slender but quite dense, and it possesses basic robust qualities, which can withstand sudden changes in temperature and dryness. Specimens from Japan and China should be kept sheltered during the colder months.

Recommended ambient conditions Indoors, in a situation with plenty of light and a temperature of 15–18°C (59–65°F). Outdoors from May to September where it is sunny and well ventilated. Japanese specimens may be kept outside all year round but must be sheltered from frosts.

Watering Keep evenly damp always.

Fertilizing In spring and autumn, with a slow-yielding organic fertilizer.

Repotting Every two to three years in spring, accompanied by root-pruning.

Soil 50% graded akadama, 20% compost, 30% river sand.

Pruning All the year round for branches; longer shoots should be cut back to between two and four leaves during the growing period.

Wiring Preferably during the summer months.

Propagation By cuttings.

Elm (Ulmus parvifolia) *48 years old*

Fig

(Ficus carica)

General characteristics A variety considered to be Mediterranean, which then spread throughout the world. A deciduous plant, it is one of the earliest ever to be mentioned in world history. It bears edible fruit. In the wild it can reach a height of 10 meters (32 feet) when growing under the most favorable conditions.

Recommended ambient conditions Keep outside from May to September; in October keep in a fresh sunny place. In winter, store in a cold greenhouse with plenty of light at a temperature of 0–8°C (32–46°F).

Watering Plentifully between spring and late summer during the growing period. In winter, keep the plant fresh by allowing it to dry out before each new watering.

Fertilizing From spring to autumn apply a slow-yielding organic fertilizer. Never fertilize, however, in July and August, nor when the plant is bearing fruit or flowers. Do not fertilize in winter.

Repotting Approximately every 2–3 years, in spring when the shoots start to appear, accompanied by root-pruning

Soil The plant prefers loose, fresh, deep types of ground. The soil is therefore made up of 50% graded earth, 40% soil, 10% river sand.

Pruning While the tree is growing, cut back the new shoots to two or three leaves. Remove the big leaves during spring and summer. At the end of winter cut off any excess branches.

Wiring Possible throughout the whole year on branches, and also on shoots provided these are partially woody.

Propagation By grafting or by layering or by cuttings in spring.

Flowering Late spring.

Fruit-bearing Late summer

Fig (Ficus carica) *7 years old*

Fig

(Ficus microcarpa)

General characteristics Made up of about 600 species, dispersed throughout the tropical and sub-tropical regions, involving arboreal or shrub-like plants, which are practically herbaceous, and the creeping type, all characterized by having a common milk-like sap. In some instances the trunk puts out roots haphazardly which sink into the ground. Highly suited to bonsai treatment.

Recommended ambient conditions Place close to a window letting in plenty of light. This plant does not like sudden changes in temperature, nor the sort of drafts which can arise inside living quarters. Keep it indoors in a temperature of 15–22°C (59–71°F). Place outside from May to September.

Watering This should be plentiful during the spring and summer period while the plant is outside. In winter, allow the soil to dry out before watering; spray often.

Fertilizing Fertilizing should be continuous from April to September, leaving out July and August. Very little in winter. Use a slow-yielding organic fertilizer.

Repotting Every two to three years in spring, accompanied by root-pruning.

Soil 40% akadama, 20% peat, 20% sand, 20% soil.

Pruning Throughout the whole year; cutting back by about two or three leaves. Thin out the larger leaves. It is also possible to defoliate in spring.

Wiring Throughout the whole year, but on woody branches only, be careful not to cut into the fig.

Propagation Simplest from seed; by air layering in spring. By cuttings from under glass in July and August, (50% peat/50% sand; remove the glass when the roots start to appear).

Fruit-bearing Late spring.

Fig (Ficus microcarpa) *55 years old*

Forest group of Ficus microcarpa*; plants ranging from 7–30 years of age.*

Ficus microcarpa

Ficus microcarpa *133 years old*

Ficus retusa

Ficus retusa *about 30 years old*

Fig

(Ficus microcarpa on rock)

General characteristics A most ancient variety, thought to be of Mediterranean origin, but subsequently dispersed throughout the whole world. It is a deciduous plant which bears edible fruit. A peculiarity of this plant's growth is that it has roots which are inclined to cling on to an adjacent rock, to enable it to gain a foothold lower down, in the search for sustenance and a means of survival. This phenomenon recreated in miniature brings to mind the plant as it would be in the wild, growing on the side of a mountain.

Recommended ambient conditions Keep outside from May to September; in October keep in a fresh and sunny location. In winter store in a cold greenhouse where there is plenty of light, in a temperature ranging from 0–8°C (32–46°F).

Watering Plentifully from spring to September/October during the growing period. In winter keep the plant fresh by letting it dry out in between separate waterings.

Fertilizing Apply a slow-yielding organic fertilizer from spring to September/October. Do not fertilize in the months of July and August, nor when the plant is in bloom or bearing fruit. Do not fertilize in the winter.

Soil This plant prefers loose, fresh, deep, types of earth. The soil is therefore made up of 50% graded earth, 40% soil, 10% river sand.

Pruning While the tree is growing, cut back the new shoots to two or three leaves. Remove the large leaves during spring and summer. Cut off any excess branches at the end of winter.

Wiring It is possible for this to be carried out on the branches throughout the whole year and on the shoots provided that these are partially woody.

Propagation By grafting, by layering or by cuttings in spring.

Flowering Late spring.

Fruit-bearing Late summer.

Ficus microcarpa *on rock, 35 years old*

Fuchsia

(Fuchsia fulgens hybrida)

General characteristics Discovered in 1700 in a botanical collection in the West Indies, this plant is indigenous to the southern hemisphere and covers about a hundred species. It stands erect and its little flowers adapt easily to bonsai treatment.

Recommended ambient conditions Indoors, in an area with plenty of bright light and a temperature of 9–13°C (48–55°F). From May to September place outside in the shade.

Watering Plentifully in spring and summer while the plant is growing, maintaining a constant humidity. Cut down the watering in winter and maintain a light humidity.

Fertilizing Slow-yielding organic fertilizer in spring and September/October. Once only in winter.

Repotting Every year at the beginning of spring, together with root-pruning.

Soil 40% sand, 30% compost, 30% soil.

Pruning Can be carried out on the branches throughout the whole year, by reducing the new shoots to two or three leaves. Trim when in flower.

Wiring Not recommended, but still possible provided sufficient care is taken.

Propagation Cuttings are easy. In spring take the semi-herbaceous growth or partially woody cuttings. Plant these in the shade in September, keeping them under glass; alternatively from seed, using artificially pollinated seed, which is sown in September.

Flowering From June onward.

Fuchsia (Fuchsia fulgens hybrida) *9 years old*

Fukien Tea Plant

(Ehretia microphylla)

General characteristics This is a shrub-like variety, also a tropical evergreen, which can grow to a height of 10 meters (32 feet). It has oval leaves, a gray trunk and white flowers, slightly perfumed, with small red berries. It developed originally in Asia and Southern China.

Recommended ambient conditions Keep indoors from September to April, and outdoors for the rest of the year, in a well ventilated area of partial shade. Temperature range 13–24°C (55–75°F), plus good quality light.

Watering Plentiful all year round, plus a daily spraying when indoors.

Fertilizing From March to September with a slow-yielding organic fertilizer; but never in July and August. Twice only in winter.

Repotting Every two years in spring, in April/May, plus root-pruning.

Soil A compost of 60% akadama, 20% peat, 10% sand, 10% clay.

Pruning Leave the young branches with about two or three leaves, remove any suckers from trunk and branches.

Wiring All year round but the characteristics of the plant indicate a preference for shaping by means of pruning the upper areas.

Propagation By means of cuttings in spring, these to be kept sheltered. Also from seed.

Flowering From spring to late summer.

Fruit-bearing End September.

Fukien tea plant (Ehretia microphylla) *32 years old.*

Forest-group of Ehretia microphylla *plants ranging from 15 to 28 years old.*

Fukien tea plant

Fukien tea plant (Ehretia microphylla) *50 years old*

Gardenia (Cape-Jasmine)

(Gardenia jasminoides)

General characteristics A variety which comes from Japan, China, the East Indies, and the South sea islands. It is a shrub-like plant, with semi-evergreen leaves and white or yellowish flowers; this being a perfumed single bloom appearing in winter. Branch growth is wide and dense.

Recommended ambient conditions Outside from May to September, in a shady area which is also well aired. Otherwise indoors, wherever it is both very bright and airy, and with a temperature of 5–12°C (41–53°F).

Watering Has a definite preference for rainwater. Water plentifully in spring and summer, but leaving the soil to dry out slightly. Water moderately in winter. Never water the leaves as this can cause disease.

Fertilizing Use slow-yielding organics. Never fertilize during flowering.

Repotting Every two or three years in spring, cutting back the roots by a third of their length.

Soil 50% graded akadama, 30% light colored peat, 20% river sand.

Pruning After flowering.

Wiring Can be done throughout the whole year on both shoots and branches, which are woody but not central to the gardenia's growth.

Propagation By layering, during the spring period after flowering has taken place.

Flowering From May onward.

Fruit-bearing From the end of September.

Gardenia (Gardenia jasminoides)

Gardenia

Lantana

(Lantana camara)

General characteristics A shrub originating in Brazil; it reaches a height of of 2–3 meters (6–10 feet). It is an evergreen plant, with an abundance of summer flowers, grouped together in flattish bunches from golden yellow to scarlet in color. Interesting because of its overall flowering and for the general harmony of flowers and leaves, together with the trunk, which has a number of small gray-colored prickles.

Recommended ambient conditions Indoors, in a situation with plenty of light, with a temperature in the region of 12–19°C (53–66°F). From May to September place outside where it is partially sunny and well ventilated.

Watering Plentifully throughout the entire year, maintaining a constant humidity.

Fertilizing Slow-yielding organic fertilizer from spring to September/October Never fertilize when the plant is in flower, nor during July and August. In winter fertilize twice only.

Repotting Every year in September or October, accompanied by root-trimming and pruning.

Soil 45% graded akadama, 35% compost, 20% sand.

Pruning Throughout the year. After flowering, cut back the new shoots to two or three leaves, taking care however to leave the fruit-buds intact.

Wiring It can be done, but it is a very delicate operation because the young branches are fragile.

Propagation By cuttings 5–6 centimeters (2–2.5 inches) in length, which have been nurtured in a sandy soil under glass. Better in small containers.

Flowering End of spring, early summer.

Fruit-bearing End of summer.

Lantana (Lantana camara) *22 years old*

Lemon

(Citrus limon)

General characteristics This plant is presumed to have arrived from Western Asia. The name is assuredly derived from *Ta-Limun*, and therefore of Chinese origin. The fruit is oval in shape, and edible; the white perfumed flowers grow singly; the branches are long with short thorns.

Recommended ambient conditions Place in a cold greenhouse, with a temperature of between 3–9°C (37–48°F). In winter, place in a very bright area, in spring and summer, in full sunlight.

Watering Moderate in winter. In summer water plentifully leaving the soil to dry out well.

Fertilizing Use a slow-yielding organic fertilizer in spring and at the beginning of autumn.

Repotting Every three to four years in spring, accompanied by root-pruning.

Soil A loose composition of 60% graded earth, 20% river sand, 20% fine soil.

Wiring In spring, with a copper-coated aluminum wire covered in paper.

Propagation By means of cuttings, which should be taken in spring, as the plant resumes its activity. One by one the cuttings are placed in individual small containers to take root. These are then put in a cold greenhouse until the outside temperature becomes definitely milder.

Lemon (Citrus limon)

Kumquat

(Fortunella hindsii)

General characteristics A shrub originating in eastern Asia, with semi-evergreen leaves and single flowers, and with a small primitive type of fruit, from which the citrus variety was to evolve. Flowering occurs only in adult plants. The fruit is very similar to normal everyday oranges, even to the seeds.

Recommended ambient conditions Retain in a sheltered area in winter but with a good deal of light, in a temperature of 2–12°C (35–53°F). From May to September keep outside in a sunny fresh situation.

Watering Plentifully in summer, allowing the soil to dry out slightly. Moderate watering in winter, ensuring that the soil dries out well.

Fertilizing Do not fertilize in winter. From May to September use a slow-yielding organic fertilizer.

Repotting Every two years, in spring before the shoots appear, removing also excess roots. The plant dislikes any form of potting which restricts the trunk.

Soil 50% graded earth, 30% soil, 20% heavy river sand.

Pruning In spring, after the fruit have matured.

Wiring Possible throughout the year. Any new shoots must be already woody.

Propagation From seed; by layering in late spring.

Flowering From the end of September.

Fruit-bearing From mid October.

Kumquat (Fortunella hindsii) *25 years old*

Olive

(Olea europaea)

General characteristics A native of the Mediterranean basin, it has a distinctive trunk, silver-gray foliage and black flowers and fruit. Depending on its location it can reach heights varying between 5 and 20 meters (16–65 feet).

Recommended ambient conditions It may be left outside all year round, provided it is placed in an area where there are no sharp frosts. In winter it should be put in sheltered surroundings where some warmth is to be found and where the temperature is 2–10°C (35–50°F). From May to September it may be placed outside in an area which is well ventilated and where there is plenty of sun.

Watering Plentifully, all year round. Make sure, however, that the soil dries out before each successive watering.

Fertilizing In spring and summer, with a slow-yielding organic fertilizer.

Repotting Every three years, in spring, accompanied by root-pruning.

Soil Preferably clayey, (but do not let the water get stagnant), made up of 60% graded earth and 40% soil.

Pruning On branches from January to April. From April to August do not prune because of the fruit; from September to November general routine pruning.

Wiring All year round, but make sure that the shoots have reached the partially woody stage.

Propagation From seed, which can be found within the olive stones; these can be preserved by laying them out in fine warm, damp sand. They should then be sown in a seed-bed and kept there in warm conditions from July to August. The resulting plants are transplanted in spring. By cuttings, 80–100 centimeters long (30–40 inches), gathered in late September/November, using strong sappy young branches, stripped of their leaves on the underside. By grafting.

Flowering From April to June.

Fruit-bearing From mid-July.

Olive (Olea europaea) *about 150 years old*

Osmanthus

(Osmanthus ilicifolius)

General characteristics Originating in China, this is a perennial plant with short-stalked semi-evergreen leaves which are also opposite and can be entire or dentate. Its flowers are either white or yellowish-white within inflorescences that are either axillary or carried at the end of the stem; confined or somewhat irregular. Further features are; calyces of four sepals, a corolla with a short tube and a four-lobe edging. In the species cultivated in Europe the fruit are in the form of ovoid or globe-shaped drupes, blackish-purple or blueish in color and contain a hard single-seed stone. This plant can also attain a height of 6–8 meters (19–26 feet).

Recommended ambient conditions To be kept outdoors from May to mid-September. In winter in cold glasshouse conditions with plenty of light at a temperature of 1–9°C (34–48°F).

Watering Plentifully in spring and September/October; in winter maintain freshness by allowing the soil to dry out prior to each new watering.

Fertilizing From spring to September/October with a slow-yielding fertilizer. Never in August.

Repotting Every two to three years in spring, accompanied by a pruning of about 10% of the roots.

Soil 40% graded akadama, 40% soil, 20% sand. Prefers fertile soils.

Pruning In spring, in order to shape the overall clipping, up to the end of July.

Wiring In spring and September.

Propagation Either from seed grown in a heated seed-bed, or by layering.

Podocarpus

(Podocarpus macrophylla)

General characteristics This is a coniferous arboreal plant, which in the wild can grow to a height of between 6 and 12 meters (20–40 feet). Its fruit which hold the seed are globe-shaped, and green and reddish-purple in color.

Recommended ambient conditions Indoors, in a bright area, and even in full sunlight. From May to September place outdoors, in a sunny well-ventilated spot. Indoors the temperature should be kept between 10 and 21°C (50–70°F).

Watering Plentiful and regular, always keeping the soil fresh. This plant dislikes its water becoming stagnant, so check the drainage regularly. Spray every day.

Fertilizing From spring to September/October with a slow-yielding organic fertilizer. In winter fertilize once only.

Repotting Every two to three years, with the amount of root-pruning proportionate to that of the upper part of the plant.

Soil 35% compost, 35% akadama, 30% river sand.

Pruning All year round for branches. Trim the candles, and cut back the new shoots to a length of 3–4 centimeters (1–1.5 inches). Remove all larger needles.

Wiring Can be done on branches throughout the year, and on new shoots, but only when woody.

Propagation By means of cuttings taken from partially woody branches in September/October and placed in a silicate compound under a bell-jar or in a tightly shut box. Alternatively from seed, or by grafting.

Flowering End August/September.

Fruit-bearing October/November.

Podocarpus (Podocarpus macrophylla) *37 years old*

Pomegranate

(Punica granatum)

General characteristics A plant of imprecise origins, perhaps originally from Iran or from North Africa. It is a medium sized tree, deciduous, with a rough trunk and gnarled roots, rigid thorny branches, reddish-orange flowers, and small red fruit. It is capable of growing to a height of 7–9 meters (23–30 feet).

Recommended ambient conditions From May to September keep outdoors, in a fresh sunny situation. After the leaves have been shed, store it away in a cold greenhouse. It dislikes frost.

Watering Plentifully in spring and summer, maintaining a sufficient level of humidity. Just a little in winter, but be careful not to let the soil dry out too much.

Fertilizing Slow-yielding organic fertilizer to be applied at the beginning of spring and in late summer.

Repotting Every two years in spring, before the shoots come out, plus root-pruning.

Soil 50% graded akadama, 30% compost, 20% river sand.

Pruning Do not prune from March onward, as this will prevent flowering. After flowering, operate on both branches and shoots, keeping two or three leaves on them right up until September/October

Wiring From late spring to summer. Be careful of fragile branches.

Propagation By means of a cutting, in the form of a branch of 20–40 centimeters (8–15 inches) in length, and 6–10 centimeters (2–4 inches) in diameter, to be planted in February–March in a sheltered position.

Flowering End of summer.

Fruit-bearing Autumn.

Pomegranate (Punica granatum) *9 years old*

Pomegranate (Punica granatum)

Pomegranate approximately 20 years old

Rosemary

(Rosmarinus officinalis)

General characteristics	A very aromatic shrub, this plant can reach a height of 2 meters (6 feet), and even an overall width of between 1 and 4 meters (3–13 feet). Its leaves are semi-evergreen and clippings can be pruned from a rosemary bonsai to add a distinctive flavor to many dishes.
Recommended ambient conditions	This plant is tolerant of drought, and of windy conditions. It does not, however, like the cold, and cannot tolerate temperatures below 5°C (41°F).
Watering	Must be regular. Moderate in winter.
Fertilizing	In spring and late summer with a slow-yielding fertilizer.
Repotting	Every two to three years in late spring, with a light trimming of the roots.
Soil	70% graded earth, 20% ericaceous compost, 10% soil.
Pruning	Early spring. Routine clipping should be carried out all year round.
Wiring	Always possible. Be careful of the older branches because these are the most fragile.
Propagation	Easily undertaken by means of cuttings.
Flowering	From mid-July.

Rosemary (Rosmarinus officinalis) *25 years old.*

Sagaretia

(Sageretia theezans)

General characteristics This is an evergreen with small leaves and a distinctive bark which, when peeled off, reveals a reddish layer beneath. It has white flowers and dark-blue berries. It is one of the varieties most suited to bonsai treatment.

Recommended ambient conditions Indoors, in a position of plenty of light, with a temperature of 13–22°C (55–71°F). Put outside from May to September in an area of partial sun. Guard against drafts.

Watering Plentifully all year round, keeping the soil slightly humid. During winter spray the leaves daily. Install a plantpot saucer, containing clay and water, in such a way that the soil does not come into direct contact with the water.

Fertilizing Slow-yielding organic fertilizer. Do not fertilize from spring to late summer. In winter every 30–40 days.

Repotting Every three years in spring, plus root-pruning.

Soil 40% graded earth, 35% peat, 15% sand, 10% soil.

Pruning You can prune the branches all year round, leaving the new shoots with two to three leaves. Prune regularly, since the Sageretia produces whitish-yellow inflorescences upon the new shoots and upon the leaf axils, and these will tend to diminish the growth of the plant.

Wiring Can be done all year round on branches and woody shoots.

Propagation From seed, but cuttings are the better method. In spring take lateral shoots 5–7 centimeters long (2–3 inches), leaving on them four or five leaves, and plant in a compost of half peat and half river sand, under glass.

Flowering From early summer.

Fruit-bearing From the end of summer.

Sageretia (Sageretia theezans) *25 years old.*

Sageretia 80 years old.

Schefflera

(Schefflera arboricola)

General characteristics A tree indigenous to Asia. It has a highly flexible trunk, with brilliant green leaves. In the lands of its origin it can reach a height of 15–18 meters (50–60 feet). As a young plant it puts out aerial roots and then slowly puts out branches. You can grow this variety simply by planting it on a piece of volcanic rock acting as a support.

Recommended ambient conditions Indoors, but where there is a good deal of light; this plant does not object to dry heat. Poor light together with too much watering can cause the leaves to lengthen. From May to September, place outside in full sunlight.

Watering Water well, but leave the soil to dry out properly before the next watering.

Fertilizing In spring and September/October with slow-yielding organic fertilizer. Twice during winter.

Repotting Every two years in spring, plus root-pruning.

Soil 40% peat, 30% graded earth, 30% river sand.

Pruning Possible all year round, both on branches and on shoots, keeping the plant nice and compact.

Wiring Not recommended.

Propagation From seed, or preferably by means of cuttings which is possible all year round, using young branches kept under glass at a reasonable temperature, in a soil consisting of half peat and half sand.

Schefflera (Schefflera arboricola) *12 years old*

Serissa

(Serissa foetida)

General characteristics A huge family covering between 4500 and 5000 species. The *Serissa foetida* variety originated in India, China and South East Asia. It is an evergreen shrub with small green or variegated leaves, with a good coverage of branches, and with white flowers which may suddenly appear at any time during the year. It also has a rough gray trunk which tends to grow lighter with age.

Recommended ambient conditions Indoors, in well-aired situation, where there is plenty of light, and a temperature of 13–18°C (55–65°F). From May to September keep outside in partial shade and away from drafts.

Watering Plentifully all year round, allowing the soil to dry out slightly before each successive watering. When indoors, spray the leaves daily. Place container in a plantpot saucer filled with water and clay, in such a way that the soil does not come into direct contact with the water, thus creating humid conditions around the plant.

Fertilizing Slow-yielding organic fertilizer. Twice only between spring and autumn. Do not fertilize in winter when the plant is in flower, nor in July and August.

Repotting Every two years in April, together with root-pruning. The roots give off a strong smell.

Soil 30% sand, 30% peat, 30% graded earth, 10% soil.

Pruning After flowering, but leaving four or five leaves.

Wiring Possible all year round. Adaptable to whatever form may be desired.

Propagation Cuttings are an easy method. In spring cut off the smaller branches, plant in a heated box with 50% peat and 50% sand, under glass.

Flowering Practically all year round.

Serissa (Serissa foetida) *flowering, grown over rock, about 22 years old.*

West Indian Cherry

(Malpighia coccigera-glabra)

General characteristics Indigenous to the West Indies this species attains a height of 3–4 meters(10–13 feet); it has a twisted trunk, evergreen leaves, and in summer white and rose-colored flowers. In its country of origin it may even flower twice.

Recommended ambient conditions Indoors, in an area with plenty of light and lightly ventilated. From May to September place outside, in partial shade, and keep ventilated.

Watering Plentifully, always keeping the soil at a constant level of humidity. Spray every day when indoors.

Fertilizing With slow-yielding organic fertilizer from spring to autumn. Twice in winter.

Repotting Every two years at the beginning of spring, accompanied by root-pruning.

Soil 50% peat, 35% graded earth, 15% river sand. Take particular care of the drainage.

Pruning Possible throughout the whole year. Leave two or three leaves on the new shoots.

Wiring Can be done at any time during the whole year on the woody parts. It has large branches, though these are quite fragile.

Propagation In summer, by means of cuttings taken from branches of that same year. These to be planted in sand, with all their leaves remaining on them, and placed under a glass bell-shaped jar in a warm area, similar to a greenhouse.

Flowering From the beginning of summer.

West Indian Cherry (Malpighia coccigera-glabra) *9 years old.*

common name	scientific name	original name
Azalea	*Rhododendron*	Satsuki, Kurume Tsutsuj
Bamboo	*Bambusa humilis*	Take
Bougainvillea	*Bougainvillea glabra*	Bugenhirea
Box	*Buxus harlandii*	Tsuge
Calamondin	*Citrus mitis*	
Camellia	*Camellia japonica*	Tsubaki
Chinese pistachio	*Pistacia chinensis*	Chinese Pistache
Chrysanthemum	*Chrysanthemum*	Kiku
Common Jasmine Orange	*Murraya paniculata*	Common Jasmine Orange
Cork Oak	*Quercus suber*	Kindai-Washi
Elaeagnus	*Elaeagnus*	Gumi
Elm (Chinese elm)	*Ulmus parvifolia*	Akinire
Fig	*Ficus carica*	Ichijiku
Fig	*Ficus microcarpa*	Taiwanmatsu
Fuchsia	*Fuchsia fulgens hybrida*	
Fukien tea plant	*Ehretia microphylla*	Fukien Tea
Gardenia (Cape-Jasmine)	*Gardenia jasminoides*	Kuchinashi
Kumquat	*Fortunella hindsii*	Kinzu
Lantana	*Lantana camara*	
Lemon	*Citrus limon*	Lemon
Olive	*Olea europaea*	Gumi
Osmanthus	*Osmanthus ilicifolius*	
Podocarpus	*Podocarpus macrophylla*	Inu Maki
Pomegranate	*Punica granatum*	Zakuro
Rosemary	*Rosmarinus officinalis*	
Sageretia	*Sageretia theezans*	Hedge Sajerethia
Schefflera	*Schefflera arboricola*	
Serissa	*Serissa foetida*	Snow Rose
West Indian Cherry	*Malpighia coccigera-glabra*